MILADY'S

FOR MEN ONLY
Styling and Techniques

Louise Cotter

Milady Publishing Company
(A Division of Delmar Publishers Inc.™)
3 Columbia Circle, Box 12519
Albany, New York 12212-2519

NOTICE TO THE READER

Publisher does not warrant or guarantee any of the products described herein or perform any independent analysis in connection with any of the product information contained herein. Publisher does not assume, and expressly disclaims, any obligation to obtain and include information other than that provided to it by the manufacturer.

The reader is expressly warned to consider and adopt all safety precautions that might be indicated by the activities described herein and to avoid all potential hazards. By following the instructions contained herein, the reader willingly assumes all risks in connection with such instructions.

The publisher makes no representations or warranties of any kind, including but not limited to, the warranties of fitness for particular purpose or merchantability, nor are any such representations implied with respect to the material set forth herein, and the publisher takes no responsibility with respect to such material. The publisher shall not be liable for any special, consequential or exemplary damages resulting, in whole or in part, from the readers' use of, or reliance upon, this material.

Credits:
Publisher: Catherine Frangie
Developmental Editor: Joseph P. Miranda
Senior Project Editor: Laura V. Miller
Senior Art/Design Supervisor: Susan C. Mathews
Production Manager: John Mickelbank

For information address:

Milady Publishing Company
(A division of Delmar Publishers Inc.)
3 Columbia Circle, Box 12519
Albany, NY 12212-2519

Printed in the United States of America
Printed and distributed simultaneously in Canada
1 2 3 4 5 6 7 8 9 10 XXX 00 99 98 97 96 95 94

Library of Congress Cataloging-in-Publication Data

Cotter, Louise
    Milady's for men only: styling and techniques / Louise Cotter.
        p.   cm.
    ISBN 1-56253-203-0
    1. Hairdressing.   2. Barbering.   I. Title.
    TT963.C68   1994
    646.7'242'081—dc20   93-39834
                                                             CIP

Contents

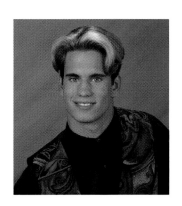

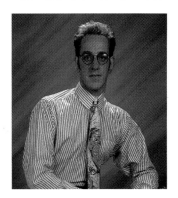

PART 3   PERMING 84

PART 4   SPECIALTY TECHNIQUES   114

Preface

The contents of this book address the artistic and practical approach to salon services for the male client. The information provided should enable you to think as a designer and perform as a skilled technician.

Your level of performance depends largely on your ability to correctly analyze the grooming needs of each individual. This text details the initial problem, personal analysis based on consultation, technical analysis based on the condition of the hair, and a suggested solution.

The subjects covered will enhance your knowledge of cutting techniques specifically for men. Included are how to subtly combine hair color with elements of form, texture, and necessity; when and how to use perm techniques to advantage and basic facts about the newest salon service—hair replacement.

Marketing your services to attract potential male clients is extremely important if your ultimate goal is to become a bonafide full-service salon professional. Make no mistake about it: hair, in and of itself, may have no sex but the person on whom it grows most definitely does. There is a vast difference between the techniques used for cutting the hair of most men and those used to shape and style the hair of women. There are exceptions. Some of the skills learned as a cosmetologist are basic to all haircuts and chemical services—many are not.

Barbering skills are unique in many ways. If you are hoping to attract a fair share of the male market—and it is sizable—you need to have the confidence that knowledge brings.

Each of the technicals was executed by a salon professional, highly skilled in men's services. They either own or work in a salon whose clientele is 50 percent men. Each generously shared their expertise in various categories.

Evolution of the Barber-Stylist—Then and Now

Until the early 70's it was illegal in most states for a man to have his hair cut, colored or permed in a licensed beauty salon meant primarily for women. Frustration reigned since many men were beginning to express individual tastes for wearing longer hair. Established barbers simply lacked the skill to deal with anything but "classic" short cuts.

As American men grew older, increased competition for jobs encouraged them to camouflage or completely cover existing gray in their hair. The average barber had no idea how to handle hair color.

Perms for men were almost nonexistent until men were allowed to frequent full-service salons. Then it became a sizable slice of the national perm market.

Several things happened almost simultaneously. Laws were changed to allow unisex services in one establishment. Barbers by the droves went back to school for additional training in order to master the skills necessary to handle this new phenomena, and cosmetologists began to study basic barbering techniques so they could tap into the male conservative market.

Many cosmetologists and salon owners did not jump on the "learning" bandwagon but simply relied on their existing haircutting skills. Those professionals are still trying to catch up to a market that's dominating the total grooming scene.

Now, after much trial and error, professional beauty salons are learning to market their services to men who are beginning to feel comfortable in a "mixed" environment.

However, there is one service that men are reluctant to even discuss with their stylist, and will never be comfortable in any establishment where men and women co-mingle: fear of hair loss and possible solutions. Hair replacement is one of the newest salon services and one that most salons have not attempted to master.

Men who once wore toupees (a hairpiece) are no longer "closet clients." They are willing and eager to be fitted with one, or many, great looking hair replacement systems. They are still seeking out hair replacement specialists instead of looking to their regular salon. In this text hair replacement experts give you the benefit of their knowledge and experience.

Introduction

As men and women move toward "equality" the more evident their differences become. Men and women have unique emotional variances that simply must be recognized by salon professionals seeking to service the grooming needs of both.

A sharp business acumen is essential in order to survive financially in today's economic climate. Salon owners nationwide are competing for a share of the consumer market that has the most stability, male clients.

To a man, a haircut is the most important grooming factor, with the possible exception of a shave. That fact is not new. It has been so as long as barbers have been cutting hair. In the animal world it is the male of the species that is considered to be the most beautiful. In our world women are perceived as the most beautiful, primarily because they have more ways of camouflaging natural features than are available to men.

Because men, for the most part, don't wear makeup, their hair becomes the only way of making a personal visual statement. It speaks about their tastes, who they are, and their individual philosophy.

While image has always been important it has never been more so than today. Modern technology gives us visual images through instant communication from around the world. Men now have a wide selection of role models.

Health clubs are filled to capacity. Many men are literally obsessed with staying fit and want to look the part. Once gray hair was a sign of aging gracefully, acquired wisdom through experience, and more than a hint of leadership qualities. That is no longer a socially accepted attitude. Tremendous emphasis is placed on "youth," if we can't be young we want to appear so. Often, in a limited job market, a man's ability to establish himself in a productive career depends on his appearance.

Men had a "wake-up" call some time ago, and have been on a roller coaster ever since. Many more mature men are torn between the desire to let nature take its course and the necessity to update their personal image. Young men can't all be put into one mold. Many feel trapped into sacrificing their taste for long hair in order to meet job specifications. Men, more than ever before, need the advice and personal attention of capable salon professionals.

The Lure

Men are a lot more sensitive than they let on. Above anything else they have no desire to attract undue attention to themselves while getting their hair cut, colored, permed or "replaced." There are salons that successfully integrate male and female clients, but who knows how many more male clients they would have if the atmosphere was just a little more sedate and "personally male oriented."

This is not to suggest a complete renovation of your existing salon. Just a conscious recognition that men are a little more comfortable in a less feminine and less public environment.

Most of you have omitted the word "beauty" from the name of your salon—a smart move. But there's still a lot wrong with the advertising you do, if you expect to attract a sizable male clientele.

Make one of your slow days "Men Only Day." Remove all hairstyling and fashion magazines in the reception area and replace them with reading material of specific interest to men—golf, racing, automobile, etc. Strategically place a couple of putters and some golf balls in one corner along with a practice putting hole. If you can't set aside a whole day, make it one evening and advertise it well. Start the reception at an early hour and cater to the man who comes straight from work. How difficult would it be to put refreshments and snacks out that would appeal to your male clients? Keep it simple and chunky.

If you need ideas for creating an atmosphere that appeals to men, take a look at department stores that have a small area featuring men's wear by designers such as Ralph Lauren. Every attempt is made to establish a masculine mood in that area.

Consider having a drawing periodically from a pool of male clients who have signed your register. Make the prize two tickets to a sports event or an upcoming live concert. Provide a large glass container in which male clients can drop their business cards. Let it be known that a name will be drawn on a monthly basis and the prize will be grooming products.

On one evening (not the same men's service night) consider inviting your male clients in to listen to a guest lecturer on a subject of particular interest to men. How about a local TV or radio sports person? They are glad to do it for good public relations. Political figures, from the governor to the local police commissioner, are often willing to spend an hour with constituents.

Men must know before entering a new establishment that they are wanted, that they will be welcomed, and that they will not be made to feel uncomfortable.

Handle with Care

Contrary to popular belief the language of styling is not understood by all people in the same way. The terms used to explain a grooming service to a woman would quickly turn a man off. Omit words like curl, perm, or tint. Instead refer to added body, restructuring, maintaining or restoring their natural color. And always use phrases that indicate a healthy virile image.

Most men are not receptive to suggestions of radical change, especially on the first visit. It is best to let a new client tell you what it is he likes or dislikes about his look. You can ask leading questions such as:

- How do you feel about gray hair?

- What color was your hair as a child?

- I see your hair has some curl in the back, was it ever that way all over?

Ask questions, but don't make it sound as if you're prying. Your client will tell you his likes and dislikes, and will probably know exactly what he needs from you.

Analyzing the Male Client

Many books have been written on what makes a man tick. We are no closer to having the facts than Cleopatra or Salomé were at their seductive best.

The closest we can come is to categorize men's personalities using the best psychological information available without resorting to a real "guessing" game.

Conservative

This man is often a contradiction in analysis. He may have very conservative ideas about his personal appearance yet be socially liberal. What makes him hold onto his very classic idea of grooming is often deep rooted. He more than likely admires a very conservative father, went to a very serious educational institution, and has always been employed in a position that requires grooming restraints. He will be a loyal client if you can produce and maintain the physical image he has of himself. Let him lead the way!

Moderate

The moderate man is hard to analyze as he has a degree of flexibility. This is not to be confused with a man of no opinion. Most often this man is tolerant of new fashion trends that come and go, but doesn't indulge. He may allow his wife, girlfriend or even a salesperson to influence his purchase of apparel, but has no thought of changing his hairstyle to conform to a "racy" image. His attitude is one of wanting to stand out as a man of good taste while deploring the thought of "sticking out" as a follower of fads.

Current

This category applies to a surprisingly large percentage of men. Men of all ages, but younger men in particular, want to project a currently fashionable image. The best way to do that is by wearing clothes that are currently in vogue—narrow or wide lapels, narrow or wide ties, straight or flared pant legs. These men wear all the "in" sports attire, from walking shoes to leisure shorts; and, of course, a currently popular hairstyle. The man with a penchant for a current image can in no way be confused with a man who yields to current "fads." This man doesn't want to look "funky," he wants to look fashionable. When he comes to your salon he will expect to see photographs and living examples of some of your work. He doesn't trust his look to just anyone. He wants the best.

Nonconformist

A man who claims to be a nonconformist may indeed be the most conformist of all. While he may reject—out of hand—strict guidelines dictated by pseudo fashion leaders and wants no part of fashion's conservative right, he has no trouble overstepping middle-of-the-road style in favor of the far left. He is the most likely of all types to yield to peer pressure. He stops short of extremism—no Mohawks, shaved sides, or braids. He definitely wants an identity of his own but not too different from that of his friends and associates. More than likely this man will come to you wearing his hair much the way he wants to keep it. He will look to you for minor changes within his own boundaries.

Artistic Expression

From the earliest illustrations of the "struggling" artist, a male artist's physical image was anything but "plastic." The tilt of his cap seemed far more important than whether his hair was long or short. Nothing much has changed where the artistic personality is concerned. However, today's creative artists carefully acquire an image that is readily recognizable.

They are most apt to let their hair grow to extravagant lengths, wear the newest "fad" apparel, and congregate in places that cater to their artistic tastes in music, art, and lifestyle. Whether this is an identity signal or a true fashion statement is hard to tell. They are candidates for services such as body waves, undercuts, hair extensions, and even color enhancement. Their personal appearance is very important to them and they don't mind making a financial investment for maintenance or modest improvement. Just don't push the idea of a "short" haircut.

Personalities

Many men carefully cultivate a facade to cover or protect their true personalities. To typecast every man is impossible. They are unique individuals that you must somehow read correctly when attempting to satisfy their grooming needs and wishes. Sensitive, shy, bashful, bold— they are all types of men that need you as a hairstylist, not as a psychoanalyst. As an accomplished cosmetology professional you should have no problem handling that!

About the Author

L OUISE COTTER is a respected educator and leader in the cosmetology industry. Her dedication to the art of cosmetology is evidenced in her life-long work as a salon owner, instructor, educational director, editor of a major industry magazine, and author of many educational texts.

Ms. Cotter's educational background provided the fundamentals necessary to communicate on multiple levels relating to cosmetology and its many facets. In addition to a wide range of cosmetology skills, her professional expertise extends to art and journalism.

She is a licensed cosmetologist and cosmetology instructor who participates in industry sponsored events, seminars, and continuing education programs nationwide. She is an accomplished platform artist and lecturer.

Ms. Cotter is a member of the National Cosmetology Association (NCA), NCA Hall of Renown, Michigan Cosmetology Hall of Fame, and the recipient of the first NCA Award of Achievement for excellence in cosmetology education by a cosmetology magazine.

During her 10-year tenure as editor of *American Salon* magazine she was instrumental in many progressive changes designed to improve the quality of information and education to its readers—some 160,000 salon professionals. *American Salon* is the official publication of the NCA.

As director of the NCA's Education and Creative Committee, OHFC/HairAmerica, she was responsible for initiating the first full size NCA consumer oriented magazine featuring NCA trends in hair styles, fashion, and positive information promoting professional salon services. After a progression of titles—all meant to epitomize the expertise of NCA's image making membership—it is now a slick, semi-annual publication known as *American Looks.*

Ms. Cotter's contributions to the cosmetology industry and related education are numerous. She participated in the creation of seven NCA Trend Releases, twice served as NCA style director and was a trainer of the 1976 USA Ladies Olympic Hair Styling Team. She is editor and producer of NCA's student membership publication, *FCA Today* and Publicist for the International Beauty Show's American Team Y. E. S.!

Education and communication are her mediums. Love of the industry and a sincere wish to perpetuate excellence in cosmetology is her motivation.

Illustration Credits

Photographers

Chapters 1–13, 15–19

Jon Thomas, Jon Thomas Photography,
Altamonte Springs, FL

Chapter 14

Beverly Getschel, Bev's Photo Images,
Amery, WI

Chapter 20

Bill Stallings, Stallings Photo Service,
Orlando, FL

Barber-Stylists/ Technicians

Chapter 1–3, 11, 12

Earline Malans Martin, Parkside Salon,
Winter Park, FL

Chapter 4

James Bourassa, Parkside Salon,
Winter Park, FL

Chapter 5

Tim Swanson, HairBenders,
Altamonte Springs, FL

Chapters 6–8, 18

Leonardo Perez, Salon De Leonardo,
Altamonte Springs, FL

Chapters 9, 10

Candi Ekstrom, Hairbenders,
Altamonte Springs, FL

Chapter 13

Teresa Natestine, HairBenders,
Altamonte Springs, FL

Chapter 14

Beverly Getschel, Bev's Hair Design,
Amery, WI

Chapter 15

Vincent Maxwell, Salon De Leonardo,
Altamonte Springs, FL

Chapter 16

Michael Wade, Salon De Leonardo,
Altamonte Springs, FL

Chapter 17

Craig Wilson, Salon De Leonardo,
Altamonte Springs, FL

Chapters 19, 20

Jeanett Van Beuren, Advantage Studios,
Longwood, FL
(Advantage Studios has locations in the
USA and Europe)

Hair Goods for Hair Replacement
Systems
Courtesy of:
Technique 19—Removable Systems
New Image Labs, West Palm Beach, FL

Number 20—Integrated System
New Concepts Hair Goods, Inc.,
Boca Raton, FL

1

HAIRCUTTING

Haircutting accounts for the largest percentage of salon dollars generated by men. However, if you combine cutting and styling, the percentage is considerably higher.

While haircutting alone is not considered a "high ticket" service, many salons add an extra charge for blow-drying and styling and sell enormous amounts of hair care products for home maintenance.

Most salons see female clients on an average of once every 6–8 weeks. A male client who wears his hair closely shaped needs a haircut every 2–4 weeks. It doesn't take a mathematician to quickly see the advantage of a large male clientele.

When a man patronized a standard barber shop, his wife or mother probably bought most of his hair grooming products. This consisted mostly of shampoo and hair creme for control and shine. Because salon professionals are capable of recommending the correct products for all types of hair, men now shop for themselves with a great deal of confidence. Men are not impressed by "slick" product promotions but they have become avid shoppers for grooming staples that have a proven record of keeping the hair healthy and controlled. They are more inclined to buy retail products from well-informed professionals as opposed to off-the-shelf products at the corner discount store.

Haircutting is the foundation on which a solid clientele is built—especially a male clientele. If a new male client is dissatisfied with the way his hair is cut, he will not return to your salon for any reason.

Unlike many female clients, men are far less likely to follow a stylist if the stylist leaves your employ. If he is comfortable in your salon, he is willing to try another stylist. Many men also patronize a salon for convenience in relation to their workplace. They often dash in for a haircut during a lunch hour or between business appointments. They are unlikely to follow a stylist across town for the same great service they can receive from others in a more convenient location.

Men resist aggressive sales techniques. While they may like the way you cut their hair, they may be reluctant to have additional services until you have gained their confidence and are quite comfortable in your surroundings. Realize that a haircut may not mean the same thing to every man that comes into your salon. Even men who prefer longer hair know they need to have it shaped and trimmed. If you hope to acquire a fair share of the potential male market in your area, make it a priority to learn as many different styles and haircutting techniques as possible.

The haircuts shown in Part 1 are executed by salon professionals who either own or work in salons whose clientele is at least 50 percent male. They each have learned through experience that men require special attention and more than a little understanding of their grooming needs. Not unlike their female counterparts, chemistry between client and stylist is second only to outstanding haircutting skill.

Technique

1

Contemporary

"A wise man recognizes the value of living in his own time."

Jack

The "contemporary" man can best be described as one whose lifestyle and philosophy coincides with the time in which he lives. The chronological age of "contemporary man" is irrelevant. Whatever his age, he marches to a modern drummer. He accepts change as it happens and recognizes the value of living in his own time.

Jack is a professional engaged in a contemporary segment of corporate America. He is an Architectural Promotional Engineer. He is in daily contact with businessmen in a position to make decisions involving millions of dollars in renovating, remodeling or restoring the interiors of majestic buildings. Jack's physical appearance could weigh heavily on whether or not his company is granted a major contract.

Essentials

Before

Personal Analysis

It so happens the barber-stylist is thoroughly familiar with this client's lifestyle, tastes in personal grooming and the limits to introducing a new hair style and extended chemical services. Jack is a regular client of long standing, a fact that proves to be of little advantage when discussing a severe departure from what he refers to as "regular." Jack's major concern is easy maintenance. Like most men in today's "corporate-go-'round" he hasn't the time to spend learning new ways to blow-dry his hair.

Technical Analysis

Jack's hair is in excellent condition, due partially to regular conditioning treatments that he accepts as part of staying fit. The texture is ideal for casual styling as the hair has a natural wave. There are no particular problems to overcome.

Suggested Style

It is a mistake to appear to be selling or unduly influencing a male client when you make suggested changes in his regular grooming habits. Your message will be heard clearly if you casually suggest the hair be shortened a bit here or there, or that his summer tan would look terrific if a few streaks of hair were lightened just a bit in the front. That is exactly the suggestion made to Jack and he agreed to a few subtle highlights. He was delighted at the ease and speed with which this magic was accomplished.

Procedure

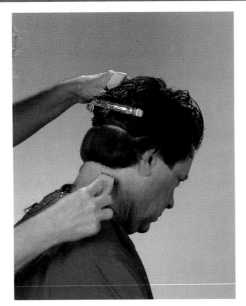

1 Establish the desired length in the back. Hold the damp hair close to the nape and cut a straight horizontal line from side to side. This line will be used as a guide from which to start shaping the back area. Use small design clippers to clean excess hair from the neck.

2 Pick the hair up from the horizontal guide and hold it away from the head at a 45 degree angle. Cut parallel to the nape guide. Continue to elevate the entire area from the nape to the occipital bone.

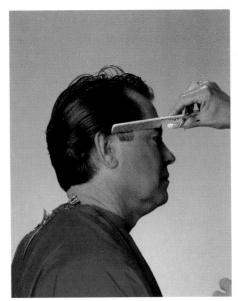

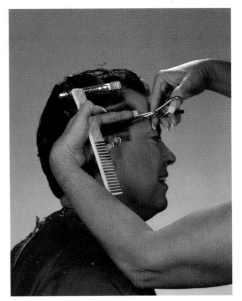

3 Cut straight across the sideburn to coincide with the top of the ear.

4 Shorten and blend the area from the sideburn to the temple, hold the hair one finger width away from the head and cut parallel to the initial sideburn incision.

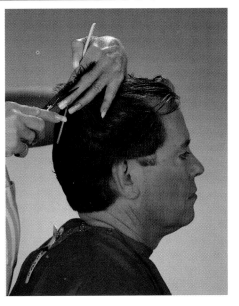

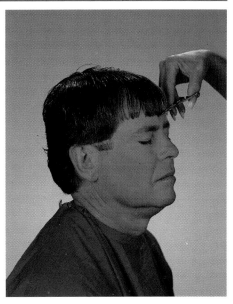

5 To establish a top length, use the previously cut side and angle a part over the round of the head toward the crown. Increase the length about one inch from the established guide. This will be the length to which the front and top areas will be cut.

6 Continue to part the hair diagonally and cut over the crown and to the center back.

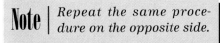

Note | *Repeat the same procedure on the opposite side.*

7 When both sides and the crown are complete, comb the hair forward onto the forehead and cut just above the eyebrow.

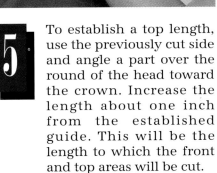

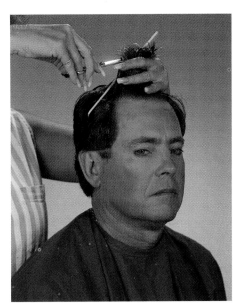

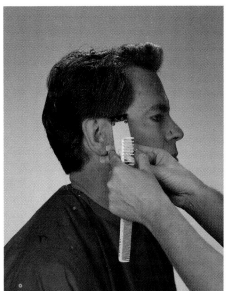

8 Pull the hair away from the face, toward the crown; pick up the previously cut hair in the crown and cut all the hair on top to that established length.

9 Clipper the sideburn area up to the cutting guide.

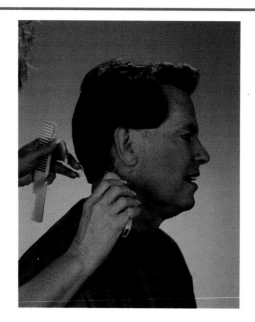

 Clean up the entire area around the ear. Blend the hair lengths behind each ear with surrounding back and nape lengths.

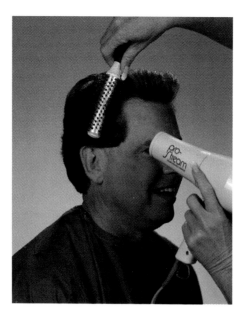

 Use a blow dryer and round brush to direct the hair into style. Use a small amount of styling gel and holding spray as necessary to control the hair.

Jack

2

Avant Garde

"Only a confident man is comfortable in making a bold fashion statement."

Bradley

T he term *avant garde* means, in its literal translation, advanced or out-in-front. However, one of Webster's Dictionary definitions more closely relates to the meaning as it is used to describe a look or attitude in fashion: "Those, especially in the arts, who create, produce or apply new, original or experimental ideas, designs and techniques." The word is also used to describe groups or individuals that are extremists.

As an artist and entertainer Bradley's attitude and lifestyle qualifies as "avant garde." He rejects a personal look that fades into the pack and chooses instead to make a bold fashion statement—beginning with the way he wears his hair.

Essentials

Before

Personal Analysis

The first time the stylist saw Bradley his dark, wavy hair hung past his shoulders and almost dwarfed a small, handsome face. In the initial interview it became obvious that no drastic change was sought nor would it be tolerated. He revealed that his personal taste leaned toward anything unusual, daring, or on the leading edge. While long hair suited him perfectly, he was receptive to a subtle change that would allow alternate looks.

Technical Analysis

The hair color is approximately level 5 with ample color variance to produce natural high and low lights. The hair has medium density and, as an added bonus, a well-defined natural wave throughout.

Suggested Style

The stylist suggested that the hair be undercut around the ears and from the occipital bone to the nape. Because the client has small features, undercutting should be closely clipped for the best result. This subtle change will provide a totally different look when the hair is pulled straight away from the face into a pony tail. From some angles, and depending on how the pony tail is controlled, the hair will look quite tailored—suitable for more formal occasions or a required business meeting of a more conservative nature.

Procedure

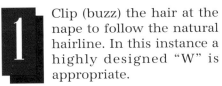
Clip (buzz) the hair at the nape to follow the natural hairline. In this instance a highly designed "W" is appropriate.

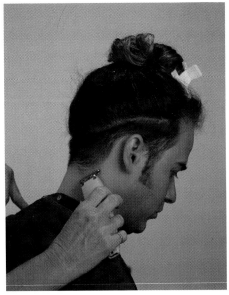
Using the clipper-over-comb technique, shorten the hair from the nape to the occipital bone in lengths ranging less than one-half inch.

To balance the bold, long hairstyle, leave the side-burn area extended well onto the cheekbone. Clipper it to an all over short length with a definite elongated outline.

Ask the client to hold his ear close to his head so the hair above and around the ear can be clipped to blend the sides with the back.

This is a no blend technique of altering the look on one length long hair. Let the long hair down and remove any broken or irregular ends. This should be done at least every six weeks to keep the hair in a healthy condition and encourage new growth.

Bradley

3

Conservative

"A realist wants to look and feel his natural best."

Frank

There is no statistical evidence that graying men over fifty are the only ones that adhere to their acquired conservative attitude when it comes to personal grooming. However, they are in an age group considered least likely to try a hairstyle that they feel is "out of character."

Still, even mature men with conservative tastes want hairstyles that reflect the mood and style of the decade in which they live. While lifestyle may be an overwhelming

determining factor in his personal choice, any number of other considerations are important as well.

Your initial interview with the "conservative" man may well be your most difficult. Most are inclined to talk little and assume much. They are, for the most part, men who grew up making regular visits to their favorite barber shop, reading the newspaper and nodding off while the barber clipped away. If the hair was a bit too short when the barber removed the cutting cloth, their attitude was apt to be "it will grow." Most career men have adjusted their tastes as years passed, but don't count on any drastic changes in lifelong habits.

Essentials

Before

Personal Analysis

Frank is a man who, as a young adult, might justifiably have been referred to as a jock. He still golfs, spends weekends on his pleasure boat, is an avid sports fan, and continues to be active in the business world. Instead of retiring, like many professionals in this economic environment, he shifted gears and continued to apply his expertise in the business community. He is an Independent Relocation Consultant who assists businesses that are forced to downsize in finding suitable new locations. He contacts businessmen in high places and wants to look and feel as genuinely natural as possible.

Technical Analysis

The hair is almost totally gray. Fortunately, it has no off-yellow tones and is in sparkling good condition. It is less fortunate that his hair is thinning on the top and his natural hairline is considerably receded. He absolutely will not hear of wearing a hair replacement of any kind. According to his self analysis he is "not the type." It is particularly important to note that the hair at the nape has a very high growth pattern and does not lend itself to close tailoring.

Suggested Style

He has expressed a desire to have the hair cut over the ear and that volume be kept to a minimum. The stylist explained that volume would be left at the nape to correct any irregularity. The hair would be vertically cut on the sides to reduce volume and follow the natural head form. He was assured that care would be taken to leave as much hair on the top and in front as possible and still blend with the sides and back.

If there is a noticeable difference in density from the sides and the crown it only emphasizes the fact that some balding is occurring in that area. The only compromise Frank made was to allow the stylist to direct his hair, pompadour style, away from his face—a considerable departure from the straight down way he usually combs his own hair. However, the cut was versatile enough to be styled in more than one way.

Procedure

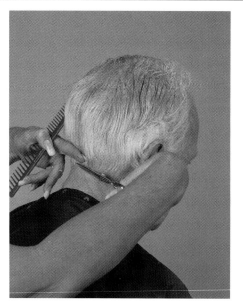

1 Hold the hair at the nape firmly on the skin and cut straight across. This does not establish a guide but determines the length in that area.

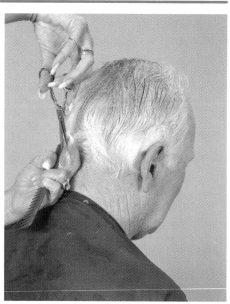

2 Part off a wide inverted "V" section at the back between the nape and the occipital bone. Pull the entire section vertically between the first and middle fingers of the holding hand; while holding the hair away from the head at a 45 degree angle, drop the nape guide from your fingers and cut from one to two inches in length. Continue picking up sections of hair; holding at the same angle, cut the entire section from ear to ear.

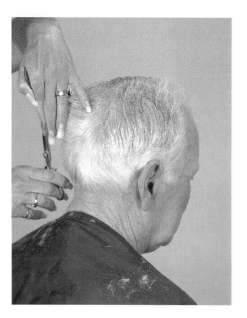

3 Using the longest guide from the occipital area, begin in the center and work toward each ear; hold each vertical panel of hair down, 45 degrees from its base, and cut from two to three inches.

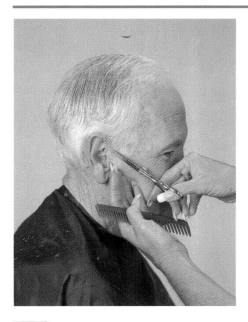

 Establish the length of the sideburn area by holding the shears at an angle to coincide with the top ear attachment. This is where the hair will be cut around the ear.

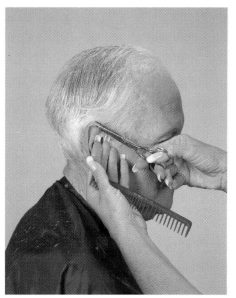

 Continue to define the line just above and around the ear. To create soft, natural lines cut the hair without tension, allowing the hair to fall naturally.

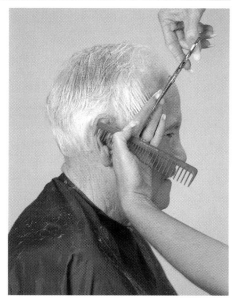

 Make a diagonal section on the side in the temple area; hold the hair forward, working from the hairline toward the back to join and blend with the pre-cut hair.

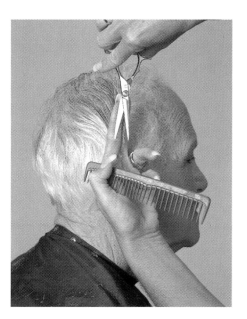

 Continue cutting and blending to center back, then repeat the same procedure on the opposite side.

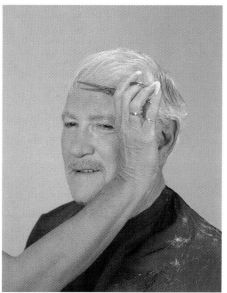

 When both sides and the back are complete, comb all the hair on the heavy side, from the style part onto the forehead; cut at an angle, increasing length toward the temple.

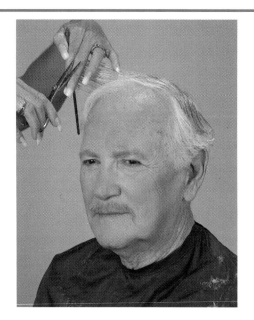

9 Make narrow panels in the top area and blunt the ends to maintain as much volume as possible in sparse hair.

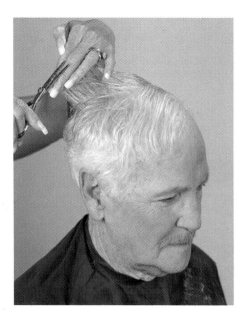

10 Check and blend the lengths throughout and the hair is ready for styling.

Note *Use a rubber-based, curved brush to apply tension to the hair during the styling process. Direct the hair into the style line and gently create volume at the base throughout the top and crown areas. Direct the hair onto the sides but keep it close to the head.*

Frank

Technique 4

Ethnic High-Tech

"Prefers a fashion statement symbolizing personal independence."

Brent

I f it's new, makes a bold fashion statement, and symbolizes personal independence, it appeals to Brent. Brent is a contradiction in motion. On the one hand a mild mannered, sensitive nurse by profession, his "flip-side" leans toward a career in modeling. He typi-fies the young, new-breed American vying for social and professional position in today's complex society. The impression he makes on a daily basis is extremely important to him.

Essentials

Before

Personal Analysis

Here is a client who trusts very few people's judgment over his own, especially when it comes to his grooming preference. He is willing and anxious to communicate on a level that will leave no doubt about his personal likes and dislikes. He exudes self-confidence and expects nothing less than perfection from his hairstylist.

Technical Analysis

His hair, true black in color, is very curly in its natural state. However, the curl has been chemically relaxed to a manageable texture. In spite of the relaxing process the hair nearest the scalp is closely napped and overall the hair stretches when wet and has considerable shrinkage when dry. This must be considered when styling. The hair is quite dry, a common problem in excessively curly hair.

Suggested Style

"The die is cast." Brent wants his hair cut in the same flat-top style that is now grown out of its style line. The stylist suggested, however, that the clipper line be lifted a little higher, to the point where the flat of the head ends and the rounding begins. The reason being, the style would have a newer look if the top portion was angled slightly sharper around the perimeter, sides and back.

Procedure

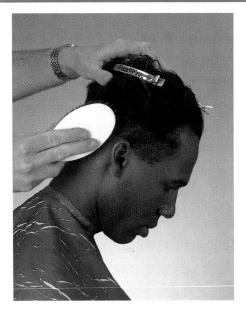

1 Use a brush with firm bristles set in a rubber base to loosen the nappy hair at the scalp before clipping.

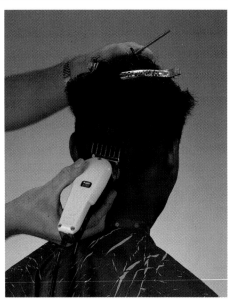

2 Use a clipper head attachment that automatically leaves the hair one-half inch long. Hold the teeth of the clipper attachment up and "buzz" the hair around the head at the top of the flat. The flat of the head can be accurately determined by holding a straight comb against the side of the head. The point where the head curves away from the comb is where close clippering should end and volume should begin.

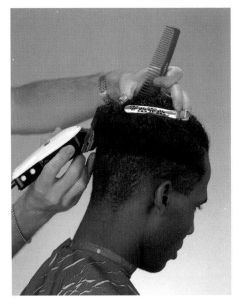

3 Brush the hair up where the volume begins and run the clipper straight up, holding it well away from the scalp, to affect a blend at the line of division.

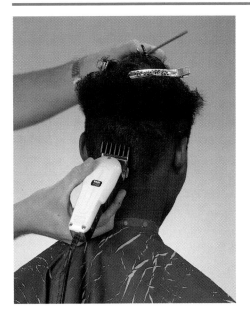

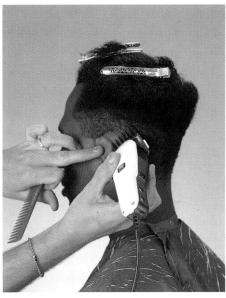

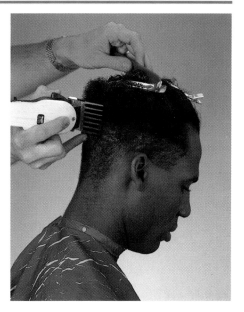

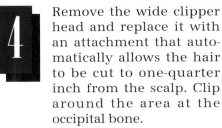

4 Remove the wide clipper head and replace it with an attachment that automatically allows the hair to be cut to one-quarter inch from the scalp. Clip around the area at the occipital bone.

5 Using the same medium clipper attachment, shorten and shape the hair over and around the ear including the sideburn.

6 When those sections have been cut, use the wide clipper attachment and run it vertically around the line dividing the tailored area from the volume. This is a second method of blending and defining the form.

7 Comb the hair in the volume area down all around the head.

8 Hold the hair with tension and use shears to shorten the hair using the longest guide in the clipped area.

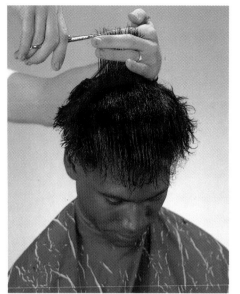

9 Make one part from the forehead to the lower crown and a second part from ear to ear over the vertex of the head. Where the parts cross pick up a section of hair and shorten it to a length approximately three inches long. Use that section as a traveling guide to cut the entire top the same length.

10 The last step in this very precise haircut is to use a zero attachment on the clipper head and cut the nape from zero to one-quarter inch to blend with the hair just above in the back. Continue to "buzz" the nape to a zero line, adaptable to the shape of the head, length of the neck, and in harmony with the rest of the haircut.

Note | *Use a lifter and finishing lotion to complete the style.*

Brent

High Fashion

"A caring, yet casual, attitude toward personal appearance."

Matthew

In the '50s young men who preferred clean, closely cropped hairstyles were known as "preppies." With few exceptions, like a modest diamond stud in his left ear, Matthew fits the part.

He is not a "loner." A large percentage of young college men are more interested in making the grade than making a fashion statement. This look is considered the height of classic fashion, neither left nor right of standard public acceptance.

Essentials

Before

Personal Analysis

It was evident from the first introduction that Matthew was a progressively modern, albeit serious, young adult. He exuded self-confidence and had no trouble making his personal preference known. In conversation, the stylist learned that he was attending college and working as many hours as his schedule allowed. Matthew's college major was marketing and business management. His part time job was in retail sales, getting as much on-the-job training as possible.

Technical Analysis

The hair was in excellent condition. It had a natural shine that comes from healthy hair and scalp. The natural hair color was dark brown, level 4, with slightly lighter shades on top and in front—sun streaked from playing tennis during his spare time.

Suggested Style

Inasmuch as the hair was already cut short, there was little choice except to go a bit shorter and a bit closer in the back and on the sides. Because of a slightly elongated-shaped face, longer hair at the sides with a little more volume would no doubt be more flattering to this client's facial features. One lesson well learned by barber-stylists, however, is to produce the best possible results from whatever hair exists. In this instance added length to the top was a favorable compromise. The tools of choice were clippers and shears.

While this client is not a recluse from professional hair care, it is the opinion of this barber-stylist that a little more length and volume at the sides would be a bit more adaptable.

There's no magic way to create fullness and length. So the client was invited to book several appointments in advance. As the hair grows it can be gradually styled to a more adaptable balance.

Procedure

1 Divide the hair for cutting by placing a comb flat on top of the head. Make a horseshoe parting about two inches below the area where the comb leaves the head, beginning and ending at the receding hairline on each side.

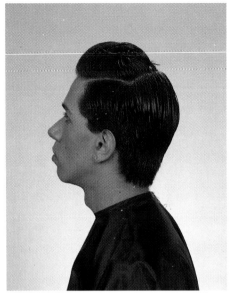

2 The flat of the head can be determined by placing a comb vertically against the back and sides of the head. Where the comb leaves the head is considered the "round" area.

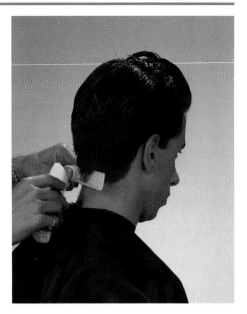

3 A clipper is the tool of choice to closely shape the "flat" area. Start at the nape. Place a comb against the scalp, teeth up; angle the comb from zero to 45 degrees following the natural contour of the head. Remove the hair extended through the teeth of the comb. This is called clipper-over-comb technique. Shears can also be used for this purpose.

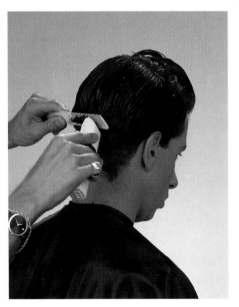

4 Shape the center back first, using clipper-over-comb. Cut straight up the center back from nape to the round of the head. Then using the same clipper-over-comb technique cut either side of center back from ear to ear.

 Carefully blend the lengths over the curve of the head. This is done by cross-cutting in opposite directions.

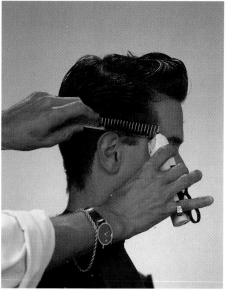

 Clipper up each side from the sideburn to the round of the head.

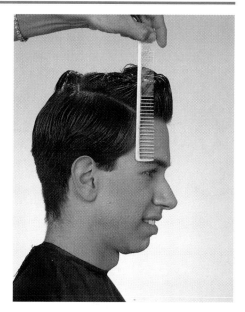

Measure the distance between the eyebrow and the natural hairline. This is a good guide for establishing an adaptable length in the crown area.

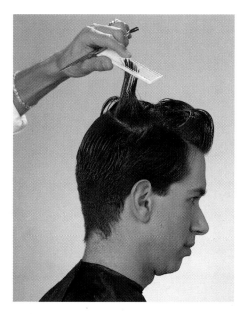

 Cut a narrow guide at the crown end of the horseshoe parting. Determine the length by the forehead measurement.

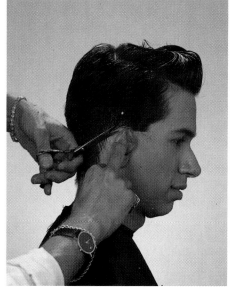

 Shape around the ear. Cut the sideburn to the top of the ear connection and remove stray hairs from the nape area that will be closely clippered to a clean shadow line.

Note | *The neck is cleaned and final perimeter touches are done after the hair form is completely established. It is the last step in the cutting procedure for this particular hairstyle.*

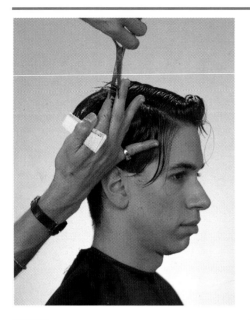

 At this point in the procedure use shears instead of the clipper. Hold the initial top-guide straight out from its pick-up point and shape the curved areas not previously cut by the clipper. Gradually blend the area between the top guide and the longest clippered length. Cut completely around the head from side to side.

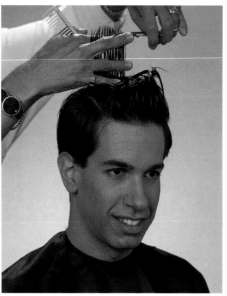

 Begin at the crown end of the horseshoe parting and cut the top area to the exact length of the initial crown guide.

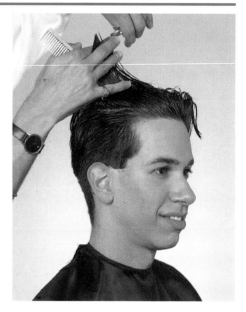

As you progress toward the forehead pull the hair back toward the guide in order to increase length at the forehead.

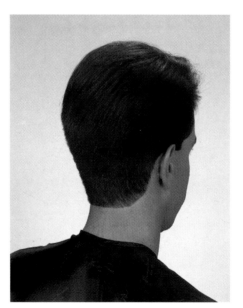

 Finally clean up the nape, around the ears and sideburn areas and check the lengths throughout for accurate blending.

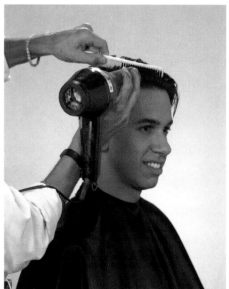

 Blow-dry the hair into the desired style.

Matthew

Classic Fashion

"A lifelong image he considers to be his personal signature."

Richard

The aging of the American male is a fact to be taken seriously. Many men, age 50 and over, still capable of holding positions in the workplace, find the career that occupied their time during their most productive years drastically changed. This not only leaves a void in their lives but often erodes self confidence and sense of security.

This type of man is accustomed to looking his personal best. Throughout his career he patronized the best hair salons. His clothes were selected to fit perfectly and give the best impression possible. In fact, he has not changed. The world around him has slipped a bit, but his tastes in grooming are just as meticulous as ever. These men, and there are many, will be your best clients if you can anticipate and deliver their grooming needs.

Richard is a professional singer and for many years has been the general director of a notable Opera Company. His magnificent voice has delighted audiences nationwide and abroad. His entire life has been devoted to the fine arts. He studied in Europe with some of the world's greatest operatic masters and after 40 years still teaches voice and stage presence at a renowned fine arts college.

Essentials

Before

Personal Analysis

A strong, friendly personality, at ease with any age group, Richard can bridge any generation gap. This is not a man who would blindly follow fads in hairstyle. He has long since established his own style. It isn't surprising that he still prefers a style similar to the one he wore in high school. "What goes around, comes around," particularly in hair fashions, and Richard is aware that his beloved "pompadour" of yesteryear is once again in vogue. What luck!

Technical Analysis

The hair shows no sign of thinning and only the slightest bit of gray at the temples and lightly throughout. Because the cuticle is tightly preserved the hair has an unusually good shine. Shine is nothing more than light reflecting from a smooth surface. In this instance the surface is ideal for maximum light reflection. The natural hair color is medium cool brown, level 6. He would be a perfect candidate for highlights to liven his complexion and add an extra sparkle to his eyes.

Suggested Style

Richard has a head well-proportioned to his body frame. The hairstyle he described in the initial interview seems to be quite adaptable. He has a square-shaped face, so the hair should be kept to minimum volume on the sides and in the back. Instead of raising a "waved pompadour" only on one side, he was advised that his facial features would be complemented by raising the style part high enough to accommodate a wave movement on both sides, asymmetrically designed to make the face appear more oval.

Highlights were suggested but rejected at this appointment. However, once the idea is firmly planted in the client's mind, you can be sure he will be more receptive in the future.

Procedure

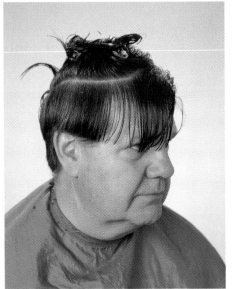

1 Towel dry the hair after a thorough shampoo to remove most of the moisture. When using shears-over-comb the shears respond better to semi-dry hair. Make a "horseshoe" division in the crown and secure the top hair while cutting the perimeter.

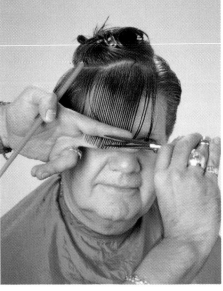

2 Comb the hair onto the forehead and cut to eyebrow length.

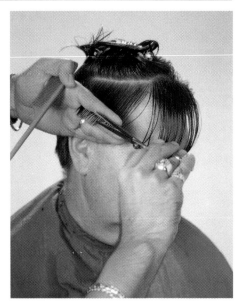

3 Use that initial length as a guide and continue to cut the hair on the side at the same length.

Note | *While the hair needed to be shaped, it looked anything but neglected.*

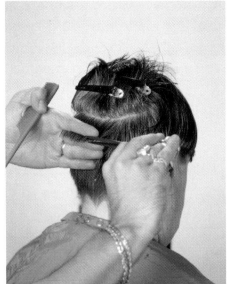

4 Continue to hold the hair down and, following the same guide, cut the hair to the center back. Start on the opposite side and repeat the same procedure.

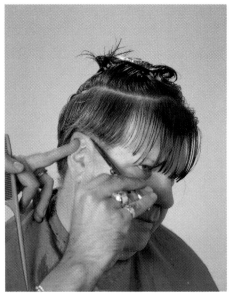

5 Define the cutting line around the ear. Remove all hair outside the design line. Repeat the procedure on the opposite side.

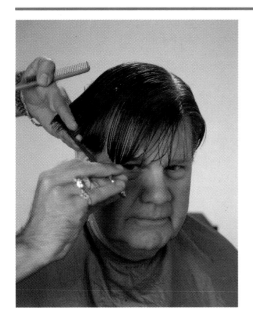

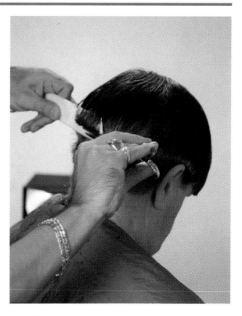

6 Make a part high on the left side. This will become a working part as well as a style part. The remaining hair will be cut with this part in place. Bring all the hair down and hold together with the original guide; lift the hair slightly away from the head until the guide drops, then cut to that length.

7 Repeat the same procedure completely around the head.

8 Starting at the nape shingle the hair up the back and through the original guide used to established length. "Shingle" is a word used to describe shears-over-comb cutting.

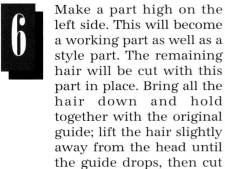

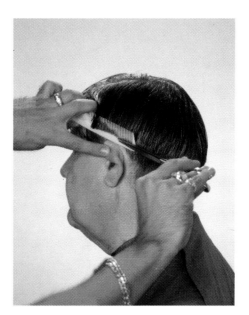

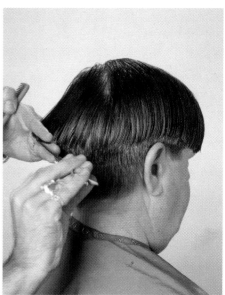

9 Shingle the hair on both sides from zero at the sideburn to blend with the volume line established with the original guide.

10 Refine and blend the center back area to remove any trace of a weight line.

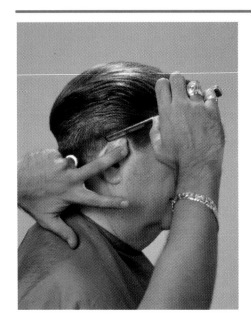

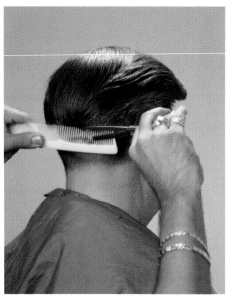

 Use a razor to clean up the nape line and around the ears.

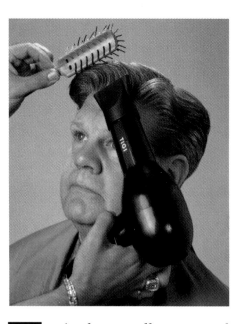

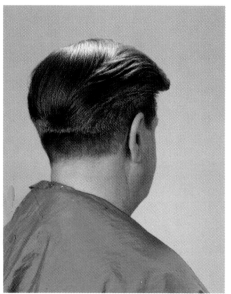

Finish the haircut by feathering the ends using texture shears.

 Apply a small amount of styling lotion and form waves in the front using a vent brush and handheld blow dryer.

A view of the finished back and right side.

Richard

Exotica

"Searching for his own fashion identity."

Phillip

Many young college students fit no particular mold. They are independent thinkers but not altogether inflexible when it comes to hairstyles. In fact, as Phillip remarked when he was approached to model this exotic haircut, considerably shorter and more structured than usual, "It's no big deal." That typifies the attitude of many in his age group. If they are not particularly pleased with the results, you might hear, "It will grow." Then, of course, there's always the baseball cap!

Phillip is American, born of Cuban parents and a tremendously "focused" young man. He attends a technical career college on a student loan and is anxious to complete his studies and enter the business world. However, where he is concerned, his lifestyle is far from "all work and no play." He teaches modern Spanish dance in his spare time. Time and money are sparse commodities when young people bear financial responsibility for their own education.

Essentials

Before

Personal Analysis

A personal interview with young men is not always easy. Many of them have a shy facade. Their answer to even the most impersonal question is likely to be one syllable accompanied by a shrug of the shoulders. This client was no exception. Good communication skill was necessary to make him comfortable and establish sufficient confidence in the stylist's professional ability. During the interview it was learned that Phillip had no desire to present an avant garde image or attract undue attention by his appearance.

Technical Analysis

The hairline from forehead to nape is perfect. The hair is medium thick with a slight wave pattern throughout, making it extremely manageable. This hair type is adaptable to any style, the only consideration being adaptability. Phillip has high cheek bones and generous facial features. Care must be taken to proportion the hair properly, so as not to exaggerate any facial irregularity. The natural hair color is darkest brown, level 2. At first glance the hair looks quite black.

Suggested Style

No priority was given to an adaptable hairstyle.

Tools and instruments used by barber-stylists are a matter of personal choice based on the results desired and the skill with which each is used. For this very precise haircut shear and razor will be used to achieve the fine detailing necessary.

Procedure

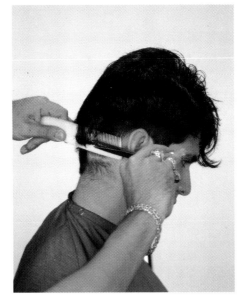

1 Begin shingling shear-over-comb at the nape just behind the right ear.

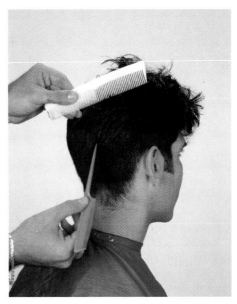

2 Using the same technique cut the entire back up to and slightly over the natural curve of the head.

3 When excess length has been removed with a shear, use a razor to refine the edges and perfectly blend the hair in that area. The razor and the comb are used simultaneously in a rotating motion, cutting only the surface hair.

4 In order to create volume on the side, hold the hair slightly away from the head as you progress up from the sideburn. The object is to establish lengths from zero to approximately two and one-half inches in that area.

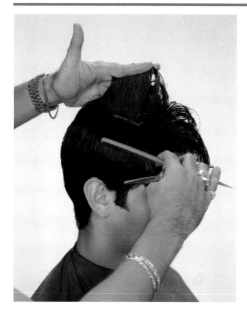

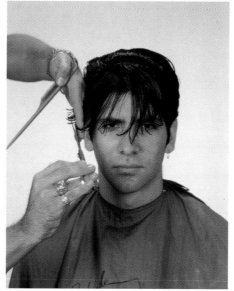

 Cut only to the natural curve of the head. When the side is combed down a weight line is apparent. This will be used as a guide for cutting the top.

Bring the hair from the top down in narrow panels and cut to the exact length of the established guide. Repeat the same procedure on each side of the head.

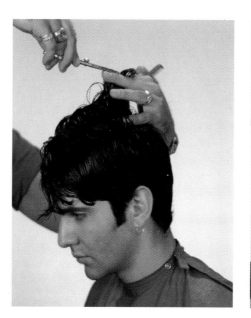

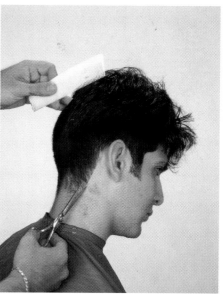

Make a two inch panel down the center of the head from forehead to crown. Hold the hair straight up from the head and cut to a length of approximately three inches. Hold the hair away from the face when cutting the front to increase length in that area.

 Use the shear to outline a precise design line behind each ear.

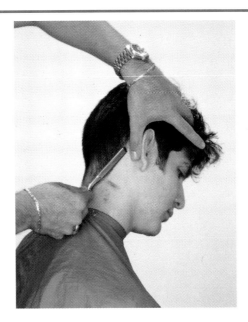

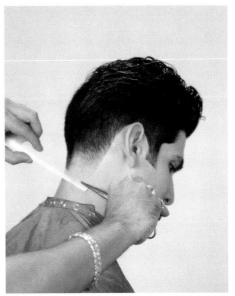

 9 Remove all hair in front of the design line, around the ear and at the sideburn with a razor.

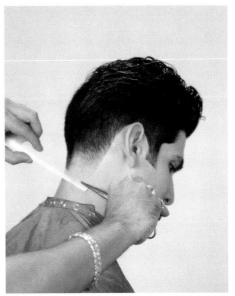 **10** Use the tips of the shear over the finest tooth comb to fade the neck line to zero. The skill used in this area often sets professional barber-stylists apart from the amateurs.

 11 How the hair is styled is a personal choice. Apply a small amount of styling lotion and style the hair using a vent brush and a warm, *not hot*, blow dryer.

Phillip

Current Fashion

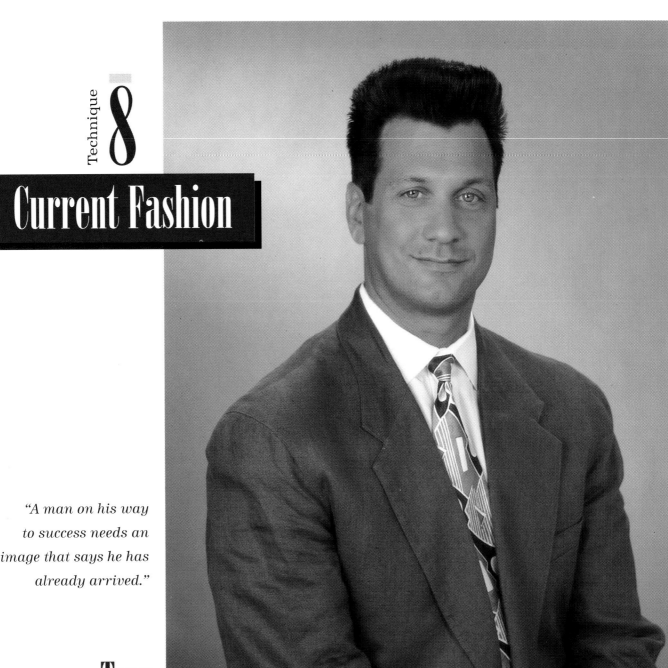

"A man on his way to success needs an image that says he has already arrived."

Tony

T *hirtysomething* is more than a catchy title for a TV show. It applies to a large group of men who are college educated, politically oriented, and acutely conscious of their obligation to society. While each man in this age group is characteristically unique, tastes in personal grooming are usually quite similar.

This type of man usually has a country club membership, drives a sports car, and is climbing the ladder of financial success. More often than not he is engaged in a profession indigenous to today's modern technology.

Tony is Vice-President of an environmental management company. He contacts large and small industrial and commercial companies regarding environmental protection, fuel conservation, and increased profit. His contacts are with corporate executives, who for the most part are neither right nor left of conservatism. His physical appearance must send a visual message of competence and awareness.

Essentials

Before

Personal Analysis

Tony is a man with physical attributes well above average, a ready smile, and a quiet, sophisticated personality. He oozes self-confidence and obviously wants to represent the best of today's "mainstream" fashion look. A brief interview revealing his occupation, leisure activities, and discretionary time for grooming leaves little doubt his hair style should be both current and easily maintained.

Technical Analysis

The natural hair color is warm, dark brown, level 5. The texture is ideally suited to a variety of hairstyles as it has a slight natural wave. The hair is thicker than average with no noticeable growth pattern abnormalities.

Suggested Style

An oblong face, a strong chin line, and a naturally "peaked" hairline at center forehead, together lend themselves well to a "flat-top" style. While flat-tops are favored by African-Americans based primarily on the texture and density of their hair, it is not unsuitable to caucasians who have the quality and quantity of hair to sustain the form.

Procedure

Note | *Before styling, the hair was short, carefree but with a definite form.*

The procedure for cutting a "flat-top" hairstyle may vary with the designer. It is important that a definite procedure be followed in order to arrive at the desired form.

1 Part off a two and one-half inch panel of hair down the center of the head, extending from forehead to crown.

2 Comb the hair onto the forehead and cut to a length just above the eyebrow. This will be a guide for cutting the center panel.

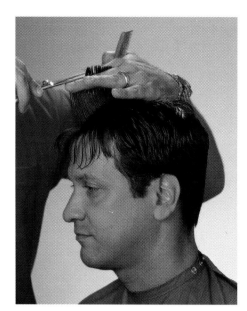

3 Hold the guide straight up from the head and cut the top front hair to the exact length. Angle the fingers toward the head and cut the hair shorter as you approach the crown.

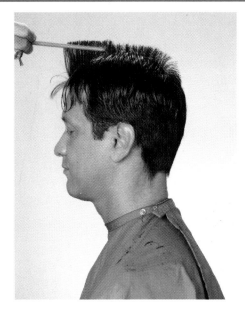

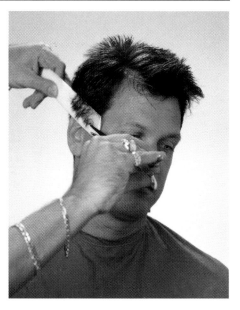

 The hair length on top is approximately three inches at the forehead diminished gradually to about one inch at center crown.

The hair length on each side is zero at the lower sideburn extended gradually to blend with various lengths at the top.

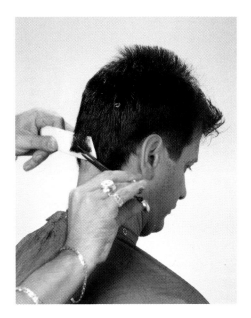

 Use shears-over-comb to adjust the length in the back starting with a zero, invisible nape-line. ⇨

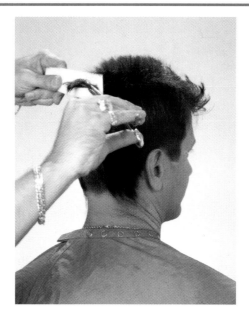

 Blend hair lengths from perimeter to crown throughout. Special care should be taken to keep sufficient length at the rounded crown area to conform to the natural contour of the head.

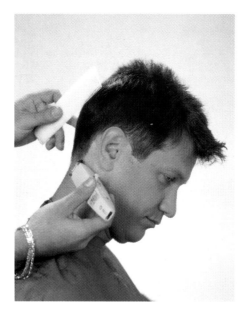

 Use the clipper to finish the neckline, around the ears and the sideburn. These areas should be completely free of minute stray hairs.

Note *Apply styling gel sparingly and brush the hair into form while using a dryer-diffuser on low speed.*

Tony

2

HAIRCOLORING

U ntil recently a man who sought to camouflage gray purchased an "over-the-counter" product, applied it himself in complete privacy and denied he did anything at all to his hair.

Even now a man, when asked by his barber-stylist what he used on his hair to keep the natural color, says: "Oh, just a rinse!" He doesn't realize that a salon professional can detect immediately whether or not the hair has undergone a chemical change. The bad news is, many "do-it-yourself" men's haircolor restorers contain mineral traces that coat the hair and continue to build up after extended use. All metallic salts must be removed from the hair before any other chemical service can be done.

Once you have an opportunity to explain to a potential male client the variety of new products available to salon professionals, and the ineffectiveness and hazards of the product he now uses, you will have a new color client.

Because most men, after being in the front lines of the business world, are super-sensitive to a "sales pitch," subtlety and tact will pay big dividends when introducing men to the advantage of haircolor.

Provide, as part of his reading material, before and after photographs of men whose hair has been professionally color enhanced. Many manufacturers have such illustration brochures available. If you use other color clients as examples, he may consider it to be a breach of confidence. While discretion is recommended at all times it is literally a "watchword" when dealing with men.

Update your hair color terminology to include words and phrases that indicate "nature enhancement" as opposed to a drastic change. Omit words like tint, dye, or frosting. Use terms like blend, shine, healthy, natural, or highlighting.

During your initial consultation you will learn whether or not he is a true outdoorsman, or relegated to a desk with little time to indulge in his favorite "in the sun" pastime. You can easily lighten the surface of his hair to look as if he is a lifeguard on weekends.

A haircolor service that shows a definite outgrowth is totally unacceptable to men. Concentrate instead on color techniques known as "off-the-scalp," meaning quite literally that the color product does not touch the scalp. These procedures are many, including foiling, slicing, streaking, surface lighting, surface painting, and other imaginative ways to blend or enhance natural hair colors.

Covering gray may well be the prime motivation for men to submit to a color service. Semi-permanent haircolor containing no peroxide developer is recommended over permanent tint products because it gradually fades from the hair in 4–6 weeks without any obvious new growth.

Keep a separate record of the number of haircolor services you give to men. Also keep a record of the fees collected from that particular service. Break these prices out for at least three months to see what percentage of your gross income from men can be attributed to each service. Set a definite goal and you will be pleasantly surprised by how fast you attain that goal.

Many salons employ haircolor technicians who do nothing but haircolor services, while the stylists do no haircolor. That is not considered the best approach to gaining a male clientele. It is recommended that each barber-stylist become proficient in analyzing and executing all services given to their male clients. The logic used for this recommendation has to do with "confidence" and "confidentiality." Men are most comfortable dealing with *one* barber-stylist, not numerous technicians in one establishment.

Keep in mind two phrases when applying color to the hair of male clients, uncomplicated application and rapid service. Time is of the essence to most men. They deplore having an unsightly concoction threatening to drip onto their face. Building a male haircolor clientele may be a challenge, but is well worth the effort.

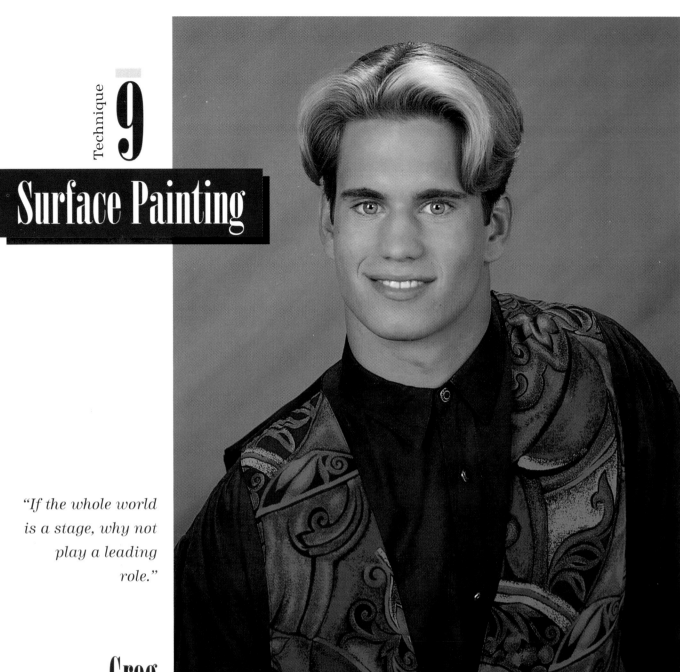

Technique

9

Surface Painting

"If the whole world is a stage, why not play a leading role."

Greg

Hairdressers must be keenly aware of a fact recognized by most marketing analysts. Young men, most still in high school, are making a vast difference in fashion trends these days. Specialty clothing stores catering to "modern" to "extreme" tastes of this group outnumber conservative outlets two to one.

Shopping malls across America are filled with young people meeting, greeting, and just hanging out with others who share their phi-losophy about everything from hairstyles to unlaced high-tops.

Statistics show that young people age 14–18, of both sexes, have more discretionary spending money than any other age group. There's also reasonable proof that their money is spent primarily on clothes, hair, and, of course, junk food. A limited survey revealed, however, that many are still recluses from professional hair styling salons, either growing their hair to great lengths or letting "friends" do the shearing.

Greg is an exception. He doesn't subscribe to "clan" activity. Instead he is registered with a local modeling agency. They find many outlets for his unusual good looks. He sought out a hairstylist with a legendary reputation to give him an acceptable "model" appearance.

Essentials

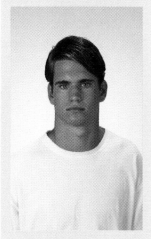

Before

Personal Analysis

This client is polite, almost shy, but is quite sure how he wants to look. The fact that he is a professional model in his spare time doesn't interfere with his sports activities. He is a four-letter man — football and wrestling are his favorites. He is not egotistical and definitely doesn't want to spend an unusual amount of time caring for a complicated hairstyle.

Technical Analysis

The natural haircolor is dark blonde, level 7, with a tendency toward a wave that breaks into full circle curls in some areas. The condition of the hair is good and plentiful. Care must be taken to properly balance the amount of hair with somewhat delicate facial features. Adaptability will be no problem as he looks great in a variety of forms and detailing.

The hair, in great condition, needed only a little color drama to make it "special." Before surface painting the hair should be shampooed, conditioned, and shaped.

Suggested Style

A professional model is required to portray many images. The hair should be styled so it can be changed from one look to another with minimum effort. Closely fitted sides and back with additional length and volume in the front area is a very versatile form. Haircolor highlights strategically placed would be a dramatic, yet practical, addition.

Procedure

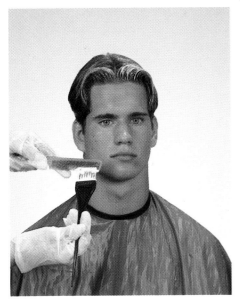

1 Towel dry the hair to a barely damp stage. Use three small plastic bowls to mix bleach. Mix each to a paste-like consistency using 30-, 20- and 10-volume peroxide. Brush an even amount of bleach, 30-volume, on a wide tooth comb.

2 Apply the strongest volume application to the center front.

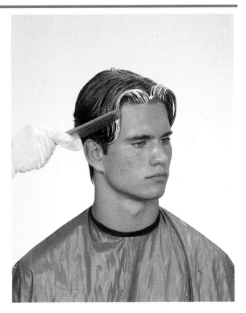

3 Using the same bleach mixture, continue to paint streaks on the wave ridges on either side of a center part.

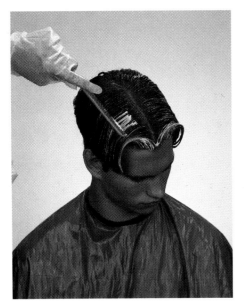

4 Use 20-volume mixture in the center part of the head. Brush bleach evenly onto the comb and lightly surface paint the top and sides extending from a center part.

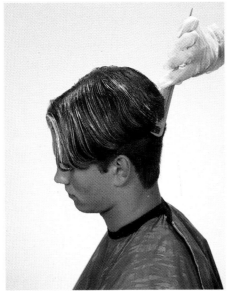

5 Apply the weakest bleach mixture to the crown and back of the head. Surface paint only over the round of the head and well above the occipital bone.

Note *When all the bleach has been applied immediately begin to test the front area to see how fast the color is lifting. With a damp, absorbent towel wipe a small amount of bleach from the hair. If the hair color is not sufficiently light, reapply the bleach and allow it to stay on a little longer. When the hair in front is processed to the desired color, quickly remove all the bleach at the shampoo bowl. The hair is then ready for styling.*

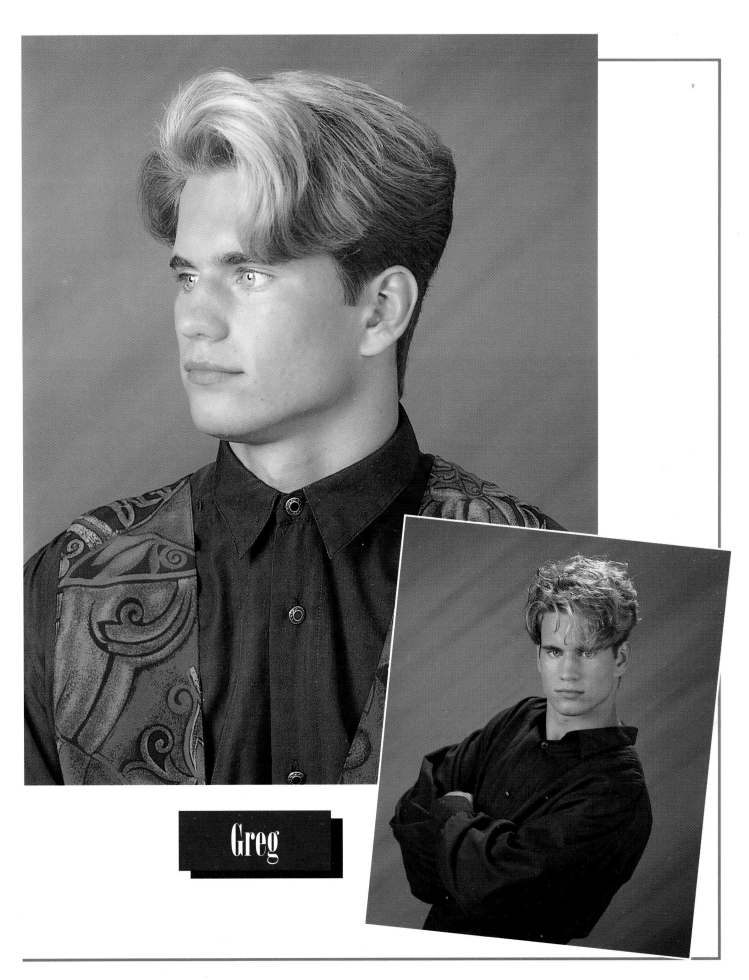

Greg

Gray Camouflage

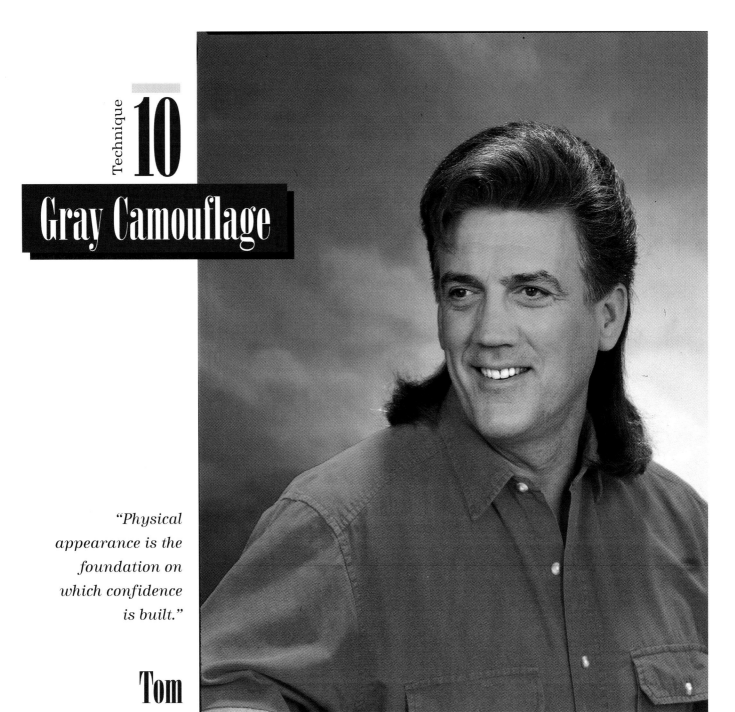

"Physical appearance is the foundation on which confidence is built."

Tom

M any men would opt for less gray in their hair but are unwilling to cover it altogether and risk a tell-tale outgrowth.

With the new technology used in developing haircolor products come unlimited possibilities. There is little doubt you can produce a color service that would completely satisfy this discriminating man. The real problem is getting him into the salon, then convincing him that he will not be disappointed again after trying a gray camouflage.

Tom is a psychologist and a published author of books on human relations. On a daily basis he must meet and talk with people who are experiencing some emotional or dysfunctional problem. His initial priority is to gain the confidence of these people who need as much "reality" as possible. An artificial personal appearance would not be a positive force.

Essentials

Before

Personal Analysis

You need only talk with this man a few minutes to know he is a realist — a sensitive man with great empathy for the people he serves as a psychologist. I doubt you could guess his professional occupation if you saw him fly fishing or streaking behind a ski boat. He is a man who loves nature — all nature. It only follows that he would want his appearance to reflect his lifestyle.

Technical Analysis

The hair is approximately 70 percent gray mixed with an initial haircolor of medium cool brown, level 6. It often happens that the hair appears even thicker and even a little wiry as it grays. This particular client has lots of hair, slightly wavy. It is in good condition because he not only has regular professional conditioning treatments but adheres to a rigid home maintenance regimen as recommended by his salon stylist.

Suggested Style

Tom likes to wear his hair just a little longer in the back than a standard, barbershop haircut. Yet, he wants a controlled length that conforms to his head form on the top and sides. He likes nothing better than to just run his fingers through his hair and have it fall into an adaptable rugged look. While he was quite set on the style, he was reluctant to try haircolor — after one terrible experience — until he found a barber-stylist that totally restored his faith in salon professionals. It was recommended that a semi-permanent haircolor be used, the same color level and tonal value as his own natural hair that still makes up about 30 percent of all the hair on his head.

Procedure

Note *The hair needs a touch-up about every 4–5 weeks. Semi-permanent haircolor products contain no peroxide developer and have no lifting capacity. Color is only deposited and does not completely cover gray. Instead it softens and partially covers gray while blending it with existing natural shades.*

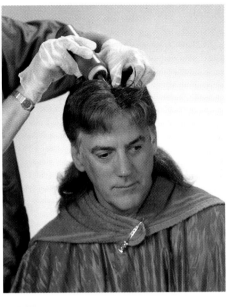

1 When coloring a man's hair make the service seem as uncomplicated as possible. Make a simple part from forehead to center crown and begin the application at center crown.

2 Work the application forward while spreading it over the new growth using a gloved thumb. Semi-permanent haircolor products are quite thin. It's important to work quickly and carefully so the tint will not run onto the facial area. Men tend to have little patience with anything messy.

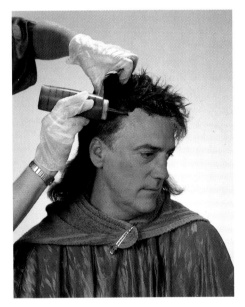

3 Apply the tint systematically on the right side from crown to sideburn. Make narrow partings and take care to amply cover the facial hairline and the lower sideburn.

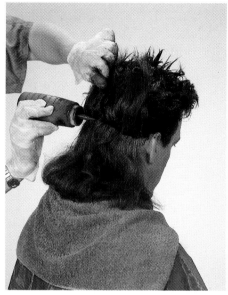

 Move to the opposite side of the head and apply tint using the same procedure.

 When both sides and the top are complete, work back and forth across the entire back until all the new growth is completely covered.

 Protect the facial area with a cotton strip and cover the head with a plastic cap. Allow the color to process according to manufacturer's instructions for approximately 20 minutes.

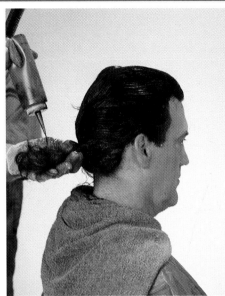

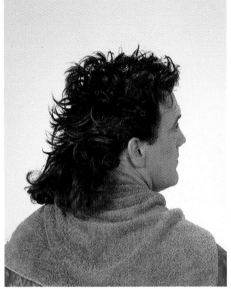

7 Then pull the tint completely through the hair adding surplus tint to the longer back for thorough saturation. Leave the color on the ends for only a brief time. If left on too long the ends may become excessively dark.

8 Work the color out of the hair at the shampoo bowl, using a shampoo formulated specifically for tinted hair. Rinse thoroughly and style. It is prudent to give your male tint client a fresh trim each time he has a touch up. This discourages dry ends and keeps him looking great.

Tom

Color Highlights

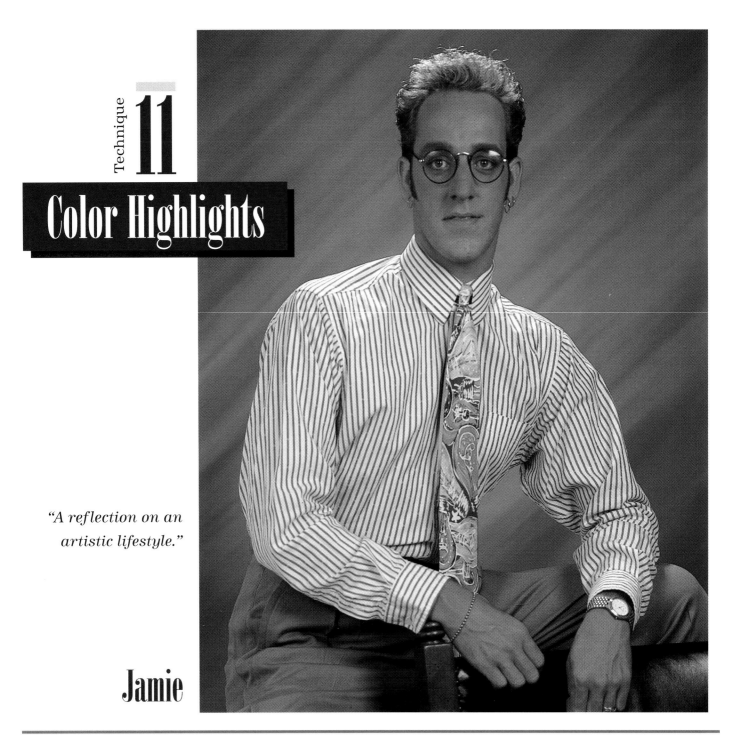

"A reflection on an artistic lifestyle."

Jamie

J amie is typical of today's progressive young men who believe physical appearance should coincide with social attitude and philosophy of life. He believes as well that physical impressions make a difference in today's youth-oriented society and is determined to reach his personal appearance potential.

He discussed his grooming preferences with his barber-stylist during a subtle but revealing interview on his first visit to the salon.

Essentials

Before

Personal Analysis

This client is an artist who has yet to determine his true medium. His artistic skills are diversified and he leans heavily toward people oriented activities. While his lifelong career goals may not be set in cement, his roots are firmly planted in the art community.

Technical Analysis

The hair is in excellent condition and has a soft, natural curl. It is already cut quite short.

The stylist considered the face shape and body frame to determine the most complimentary length. She carefully explained exactly what style she had in mind.

Suggested Style

It was suggested the hair be cut very short on the sides and in the back and that the natural curl be emphasized on the top. It was the opinion of the stylist that Jamie's features would be softened by highlighting his natural haircolor, level 6, by means of foiling to a complimentary amount of level 9.

Note: It is important to explain to male clients step-by-step how the color service will be done. Unlike women, most men have no experience with professional salon haircoloring services. Jamie's stylist explained that narrow sections of hair would be isolated; a narrow piece of foil would be placed under the section; fast-action bleach brushed onto the hair strands; the foil strip folded and processed for approximately ten minutes. Eighteen such sections should sufficiently cover the entire crown, front, and natural round of the head.

Procedure

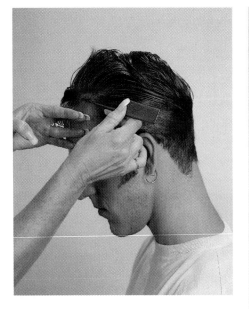

1 Start at one side along the curve of the head. This occurs from mid-eyebrow to temple.

Note | *This is a slicing technique with the exception of the hairline. By weaving out minute strands to be left unbleached at the hairline you will achieve a natural looking blend that frames the face.*

Make an angular slice approximately one-quarter inch wide. The width of the slice depends on the density of the hair and the desired amount of lightness. If the hair is very thick, the slices should still be kept narrow, but more may be needed to reach the desired level of lightness.

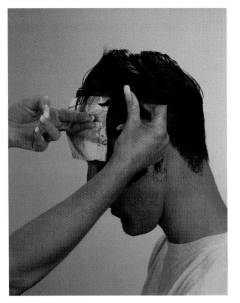

2 Place a pre-cut strip of foil under the entire section, held firmly in place at the scalp with a tail comb.

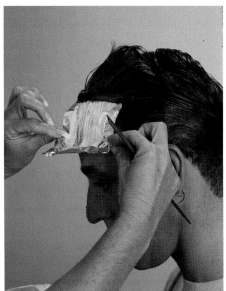

3 Apply a sufficient amount of bleach to cover the hair strands. *Do not* allow the bleach to touch the head. If the bleach application is too heavy the bleach is apt to seep onto the scalp.

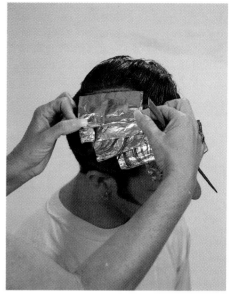

 Fold the foil toward the scalp to make a protective pocket. *Do not* squeeze or flatten the pocket or the bleach might seep from the sides or at the scalp.

 When one side is finished repeat the procedure on the opposite side.

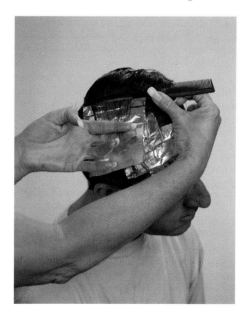

 Slice and foil the hair over the round of the head under the crown to blend into the occipital and nape area. ⇨

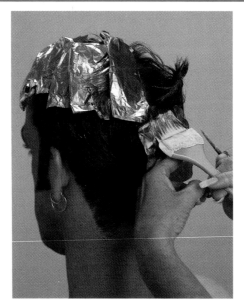

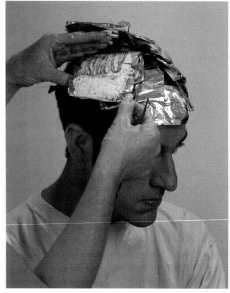

 Pre-heat a dryer to about 135° F. Place the client with foils intact under the dryer and begin testing for desired lift.

 When the hair has lightened to the desired level take the client to the shampoo bowl and quickly remove all the foils. Rinse the hair well in tepid water and follow with a conditioning shampoo. *Do not* attempt to apply a toner or rinse over the bleached strands. None is necessary. Style the hair as determined in the initial consultation.

Jamie

PERMING

alk "body," not "curl" to your male clients, unless of course, *curl* is his idea. Never promote any service for the sake of extra money. Your true motivation for selling additional services to clients, who regularly come in for a trim, should always be for the client's benefit. That's not to say that inadvertently you will not also benefit. You certainly will.

Men are not unlike women, inasmuch as few are totally satisfied with the hair nature gave them. It's either too straight, too curly, too thin or occasionally too much.

Chemically restructuring hair texture is called "permanent wave." Progressive salon professionals now refer to it only as a *perm*, but like a bad reputation it's hard to change old attitudes if the name is the same. Many men have either had a bad perm experience once in their life, or they know someone who has. That alone makes them less likely to try that same service again.

It is up to you to convince the client that his appearance would be improved by chemical restructuring. You must overcome any negative ideas he may have. It's important that you use a "gentler" vocabulary when talking to men about a perm. Observe that their hair has very little body and no bounce because it is fine and limp; talk about his cow-lick that wants to go its own way or sticks straight up when the hair is cut short. A perm only at the scalp would do wonders to correct both problems.

Some men have receding hairlines or the awful realization that male pattern baldness may be in their near future. A body perm can camouflage both problems. The real problem of noticeable hair loss can be postponed.

You should carefully consider the price of a perm service to your male clients. While a man is less likely than a woman to consider the price when making a purchase, he still likes to feel he is getting his money's worth. A man who wears his hair short in the back and on the sides needs fewer perm rods and less product than the client whose hair is long. Adjust your prices to reflect the difference.

I'm sure you've dined at a fine restaurant where the host was the only person at the table whose menu had a price list. Take a cue from that practice and give your male clients a personal and private menu of services exclusively for him. Men hate to ask the price of anything, much less a haircare service. They haven't enough experience to know if the price is fair. Provide him with a complete list of services specifically for men, including the options.

Try not to fragment the price of a perm. Men like to see what the bottom line will be. Let it show on the price list that a perm includes shaping and styling. You can factor those services in yourself. There's no reason to confuse them. It is suggested as well that you show a price for various lengths of hair. It's a waste of time to mention such options as "deluxe, super moisturized or standard." That will only prompt them to ask you to explain the difference. It sounds like a sales gimmick, a way of raising the price to whatever the traffic will bear. Let your clients know that the real difference in a perm service lies in the knowledge and skill of the technician and that your salon provides only first quality service under all conditions.

Be prepared to do the final haircut after the perm is complete. Shaping the hair after it is chemically texturized will blend all areas, remove extreme ends that might have curled too tight or too loose and create a look of natural movement.

There's more than one reason why men patronize professional, full service salons, but the principal reason is that they want to look their best. They have been led to believe, either by experience, by advertising or by word of mouth, that you can deliver the goods.

Never forget he is there to improve his appearance and to make styling his hair easier. He wants hair that is full and easily controlled with the least amount of effort. You know a perm would help. All you have to do is convince him of something he's anxious to believe in the first place.

12

Subtle Change

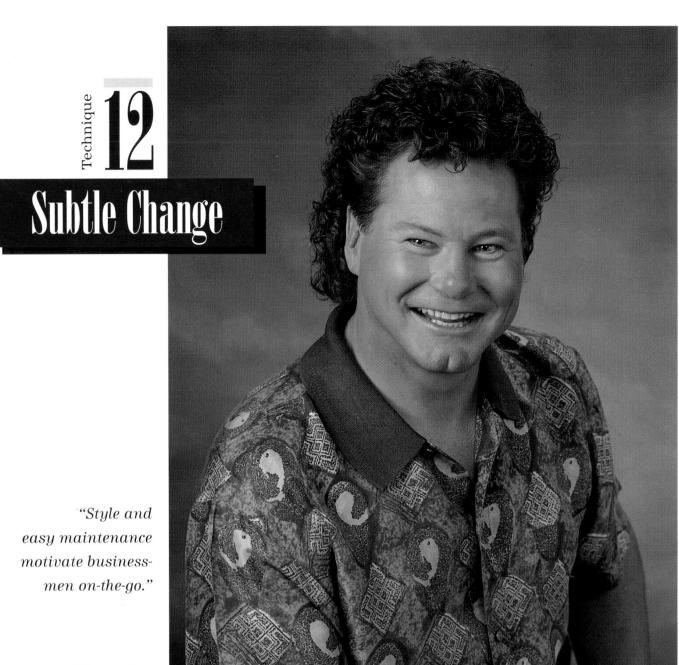

"Style and easy maintenance motivate business-men on-the-go."

Timothy

Men have slowly learned what women have known throughout history, that hair texture, whether the hair is curly or straight, determines the limitation of styling options. Today's technology allows subtle structural changes that replicate nature. Sophisticated men, in increasing numbers, are opting for a perm.

Timothy is the epitome of modern business moguls. He was not born to wealth but attained both wealth and international respect through wit, business acumen and perseverance. His import-export activities require him to jet from Hong Kong to the Far East at a moment's notice. He requires a hairstyle that is always right for any occasion. A perm gives him that freedom.

Essentials

Before

Personal Analysis

A short interview revealed Tim as an aggressive, charismatic entrepreneur. He relies on physical appearance and personality to span language barriers and make a positive impression on the most conservative and wily business contact. He does not want to appear vain or artificial. His success often depends on straightforward confidence. His motto is, "Look a man straight in the eye and give him a 'firm' handshake."

Technical Analysis

This client's hair is plentiful but medium fine. There are slight signs of a receding hairline. His facial features are full and youthful. The hair color is light medium brown, level 6, and in fair condition considering the time he spends in outdoor activities.

Suggested Style

There's no doubt the hair needs textural control. The need for adaptability is just as obvious. The overall body structure of a man plays a major role in selecting a suitable hairstyle. The hair should be left a sufficient length to hang loosely just above his suit collar. For a more controlled look it can be pulled back into a short pony tail. To cover a high forehead the hair in front should be of a length and curl structure to give softness and a bit of camouflage.

Procedure

This was not a virgin perm. However, it has been more than three months since Tim's last perm and the hair needs to be restructured and shaped.

Shampoo the hair and remove excess water. The hair will be wrapped in a "brick-laying" pattern, making pre-sectioning unnecessary. The desired curl determines the size of the rod. In this case a soft, open end curl is expected as an end result. A perm rod with a medium diameter is selected for use throughout.

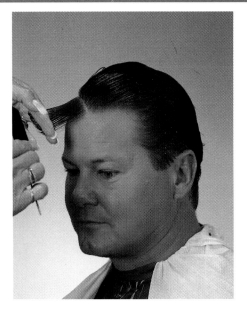

1 Make a diagonal section, equal to the width and length of the perm rod, slightly off the center of the forehead. Comb the hair forward in preparation to position an "over-directed" rod half off its base.

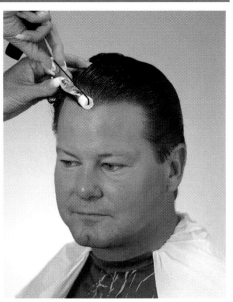

2 Use two end papers and wrap the rod from end to scalp. Be sure to pull the rubber band on the perm rod straight across and on top of the rod. Any twisting of the band may cause excess tension making breakage a possibility.

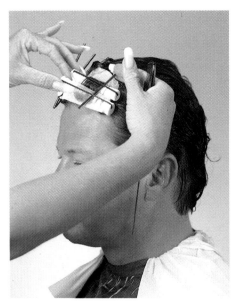

3 Wrap the front area, sectioning and wrapping from side to side, then slide non-porous plastic picks under the rubber bands of two or three rods to hold them firmly in place.

4 Increase the width of each section in the crown. Hold the hair straight up. Comb the entire strand through from scalp to ends.

 Protect the hair by placing an end paper underneath and on top of the strand.

Wrap the hair using medium tension and position the rod on-base.

The front, crown and back—to the occipital bone—are considered the basis areas for maximum structural change.

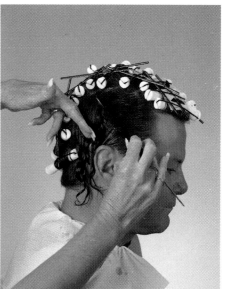

The sides, the area above each ear, and the nape are wrapped using "V" shaped partings for definite direction. These areas are also wrapped without tension to effect soft, manageable movement. ⇨

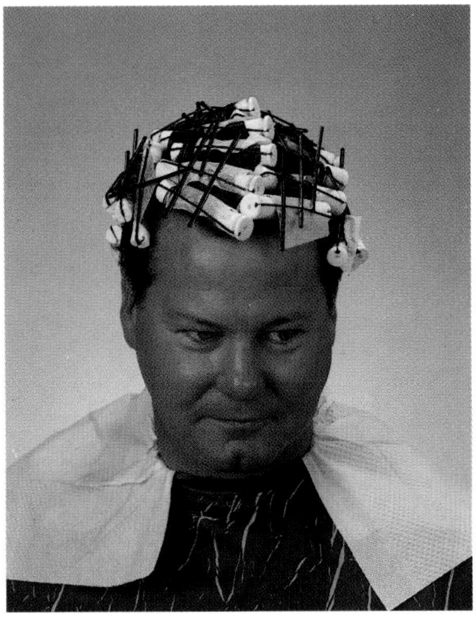

9 Completed perm wrap — front view.

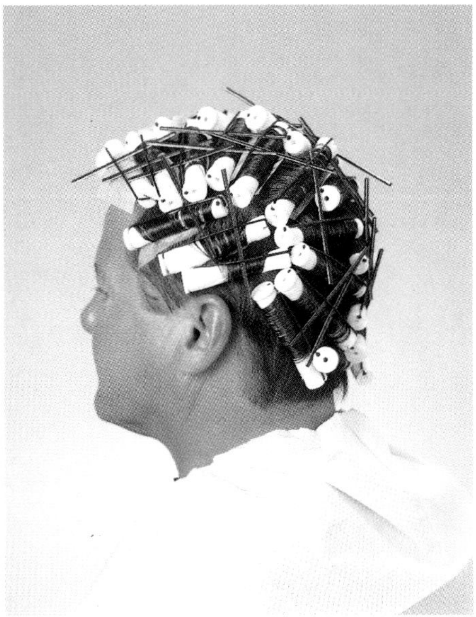

10 Completed perm wrap — side view.

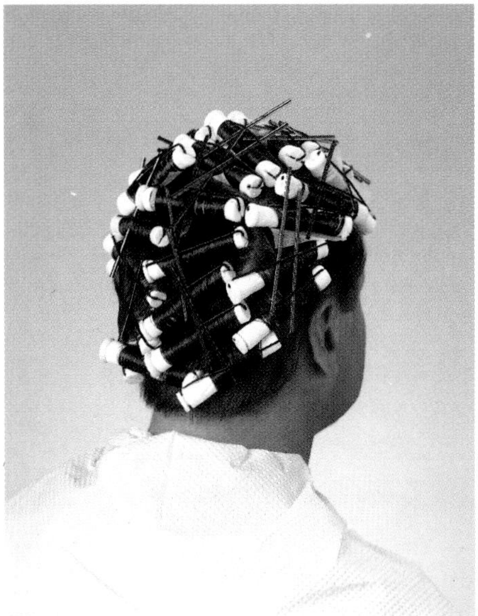

11 Completed perm wrap — back view.

12 Completed perm — unstyled.

Note *Process and neutralize the perm according to manufacturer's instructions. Towel dry and shape to style.*

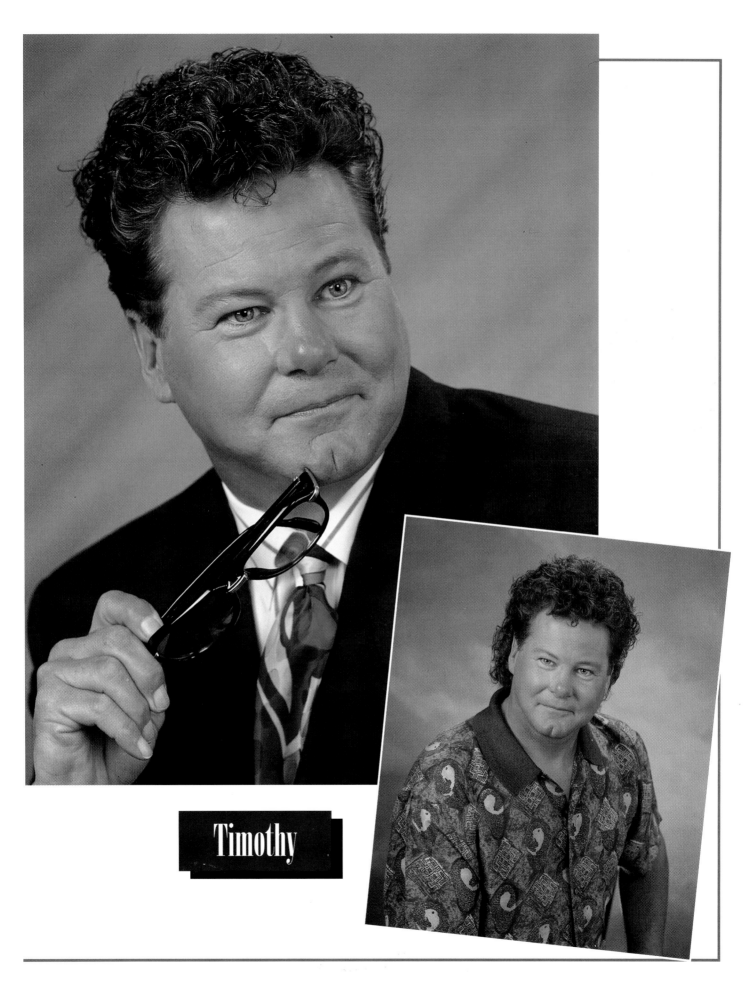

Timothy

Spot Perming

"Freedom of choice often encourages versatility."

Charles

Charles, for many years, stifled his own personal taste in appearance to conform to the strict dress code of his employers. When he went into business for himself he lost no time in exercising his right to dress any way he pleased. Above all he was determined to wear his hair as long or as short as he saw fit.

Charles owns an impressive landscape company that caters specifically to large, exclusive estates. While he can, with discretion, dress in a manner commensurate with his occupation,

he is careful to make a favorable impression on his wealthy and often conservative customers.

Men who are in a position to choose their own personal style, often experiment with hairstyles more liberal than would be tolerated in a structured business environment. This by no means brands them as renegades. They simply enjoy the optional look that can be achieved with longer hair.

Essentials

Before

Personal Analysis

This client was a good communicator and there was no evidence of an overinflated ego. His personality left no doubt that his lifestyle was one of masculine adventure. Fishing, hiking, hunting or just hanging out with the boys was his idea of relaxation. Long hair would in no way diminish that character.

Technical Analysis

The natural hair color was medium blonde with natural highlights caused from working in the sun. The hair was somewhat dry and could benefit from a conditioning treatment. The hair had a slight natural wave movement that was weighted down for lack of shaping.

Suggested Style

The stylist explained that the hair would look fuller and have a much healthier appearance if given a spiral perm in the back. The front should be shaped and shortened to create a contrast between the two areas. The hair would be easier to handle if it was softly layered in the long areas and the long and short hair well blended behind each ear.

Procedure

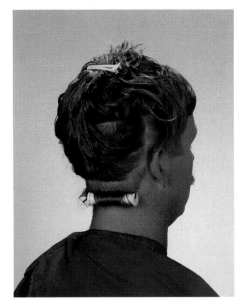

1 There is no pre-sectioning necessary as a back-and-forth pattern is followed throughout to effect a natural blend in the completed perm. Clip all but a one inch section of hair up and out of the way. Position three horizontal, on-base rods across the nap area.

2 Let down another horizontal section of hair from ear to ear. The width of each section depends on the density of the hair. Approximately one and one half inch sections are used for this client. Begin wrapping at either side. Part off a strand of hair from the horizontal section. Hold the hair down at about 45 degrees. Apply a single end paper to the end of the strand.

3 Wrap one complete circle of hair inside the end paper.

 From that point turn the rod toward the scalp so the hair spirals around the rod.

 While holding the hair and the rod with sufficient tension to keep the hair ribboned, continue to turn the rod all the way to the scalp. Carefully secure the rod by attaching the rubber band from top to bottom.

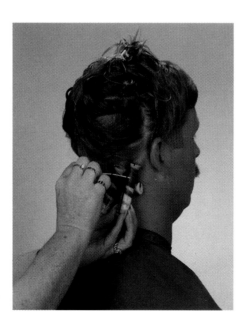

To hold the rod in position slide a plastic pick under the band.

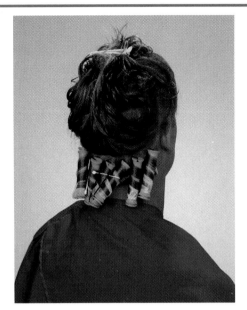

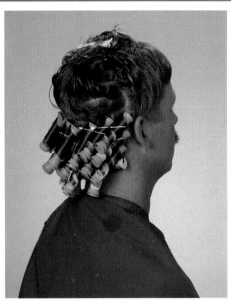

 The first completed spiral section.

 Continue to let down one and one-half to two inch horizontal sections from side to side. Use the same spiral wrapping technique on each section. Position each perm rod to lay between two previously wrapped rods creating a wrap with no empty spaces and no rods on top of each other.

 When all but the crown section is spirally wrapped place a vertical on-base rod directed away from the face at the division line, between sides and back. This helps effect a blend in that area.

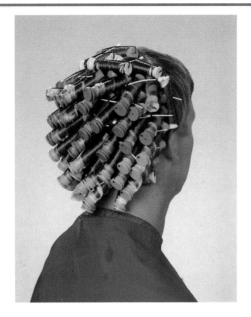

 Use a standard "brick-laying" pattern in the crown area for blend, front to back, and a bit of volume.

 Side view of the finished wrap. All the hair in the back is wrapped from the nape to a division line ear to ear across the crest of the head.

 Three-quarter view of the finished wrap from the opposite side. ⇨

Note *Process the hair according to manufacturer's instructions. Test the progress of the curl by partially unspiralling a rod in more than one area of the head. When the unwound hair, held without tension, shows a strong tendency to bend into a half circle the perm is sufficiently processed. Rinse and neutralize the hair on the rod.*

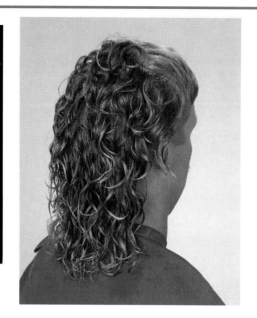

13 The completed perm; rods removed and excess moisture blotted with a soft towel. The hair may be styled by applying a styling aid and allowing it to dry naturally, or it can be dried using a diffuser for a fuller, more curly style.

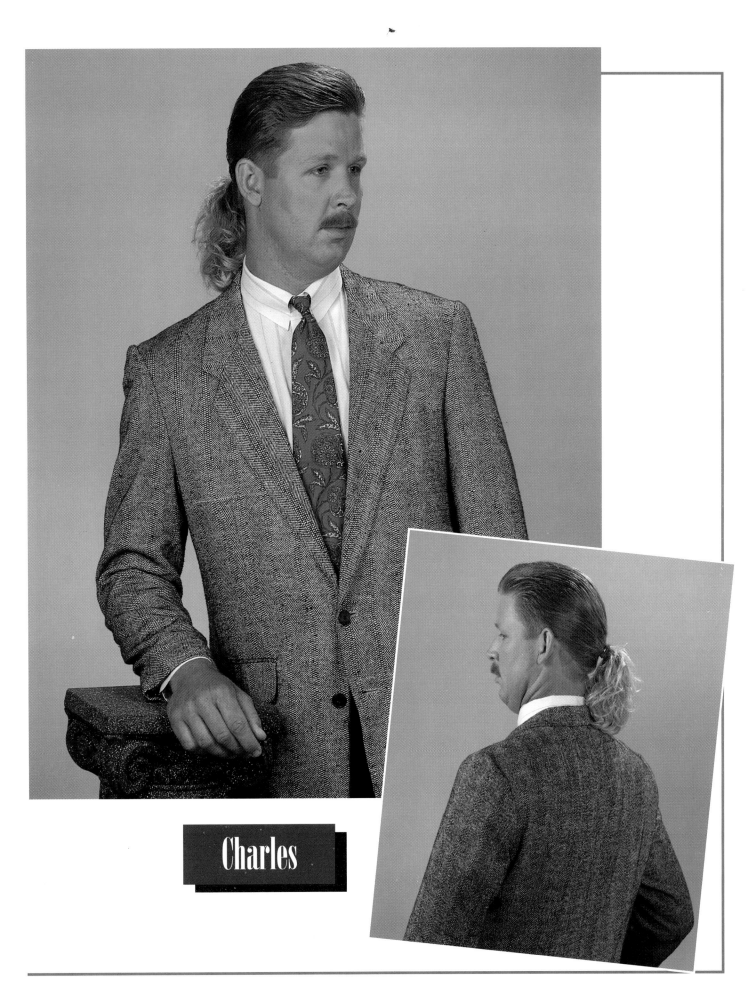

Charles

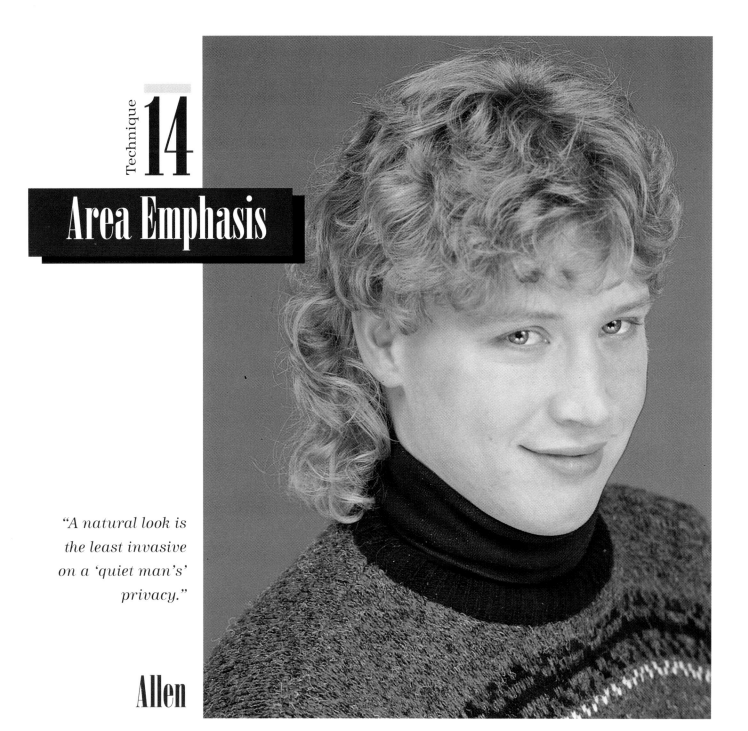

Area Emphasis

"A natural look is the least invasive on a 'quiet man's' privacy."

Allen

There's a certain type of man that is simply unwilling to wear a hairstyle that looks artificial. He may have once had a perm that is entrenched in his mind forever. He either wore a hat for several months or opted for a very short haircut to rid himself of the "Shirley Temple" look.

He's more than anxious to get the salon service that would change his "almost straight, somewhat sparse" hair to full, natural looking waves. But he wants the result to look as if it was provided by Mother Nature.

You must, in the initial consultation, gain his confidence as a professional. Never promise more than you can deliver. Someone who has had a bad salon experience is not easily sold on taking another chance.

Often the underlying fear of looking artificially groomed stems from a reluctance to compromise the "all natural" male image that he holds of himself. To help overcome that problem hand him a style book showing strong, athletic men before and after a perm service. That usually does it.

Allen is an entrepreneur. How he wears his hair is dictated only by his own taste. He dislikes the reality that his hair is showing signs of receding at the front hairline. While it is not particularly noticeable to anyone but him, he is anxious to see what additional volume and change of texture will do in that area.

Essentials

Before

Personal Analysis

This is a sensitive man who values his privacy. He is an avid sports enthusiast and coaches a Little League baseball team. He is a dedicated family man with a young daughter and a new son. He has absolutely no discretionary time to spend on personal grooming. Every hair simply must fall naturally in place.

Technical Analysis

The hair color is medium blonde, level 7, with a slight but uncontrollable wave movement. The hair has a tendency to part in the middle and fall forward onto the forehead. The density throughout is uneven. The hair is much thicker in the back than it is in the front. It is unlikely that a chemical perm would change some of the natural directional tendencies, but added volume would provide more coverage at the hairline.

Suggested Style

It is rather obvious that Allen wants to keep his hair at a medium length. It's just as obvious to the professional eye that the hair will not be improved by shaping alone. An all-over permanent wave followed by a good shaping would make a positive difference.

Procedure

The Perm

1 Before styling there was rather obvious room for improvement. Section the hair in preparation for the perm using as few holding clips as possible.

Note *When perming the hair of a male client, make the service, especially the preparation, as simple as possible.*

2 Position one large diameter perm rod, on-base, in the center of the forehead. Direct the rod forward.

3 Make subsections the width and length of each rod. Use medium diameter rods in the front area. Direct all rods forward from center crown to front hairline. Position each rod on-base for maximum lift.

4 Divide the back into three sections, each as wide as the length of the perm rod.

5 Start at the crown and wrap the center back section down toward the nape. Position each medium diameter rod above the occipital bone directly on base. At that point switch to a larger diameter rod and position the rods half off-base.

6 Follow the same procedure to wrap the two remaining back sections. Place plastic picks under the rubber bands to hold the perm rods in place.

Note | *If the hair is fragile, place picks at the ends of the rods, not resting on the hair.*

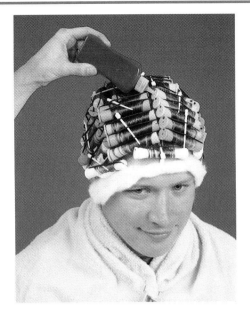

7 When the wrap is completed protect the hairline with a cotton strip and apply perm lotion on top and inside each perm rod. Be sure all the hair wrapped around each rod is thoroughly saturated.

Note *Process and neutralize the perm according to manufacturer's instructions.*

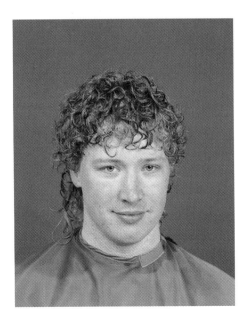

8 After neutralizing is complete carefully remove the rods and rinse the hair thoroughly.

The Cut

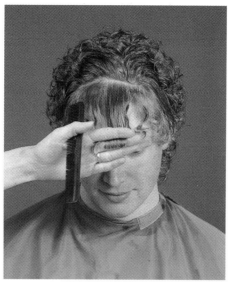

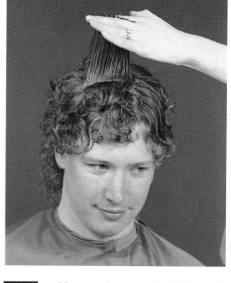

 Because a man's hair is already short, it is best to give a final hair shaping after the perm is complete. This may be done wet or dry. Considering the perm was given to camouflage a sparse hairline the first thing you must do is make sure the hair around the face frame is long enough to create the movement and volume to accomplish this goal. Comb the hair forward and cut to eyebrow length.

Use the established guide to gauge the length on top and crown. Cut a center panel approximately three inches wide from forehead to crown.

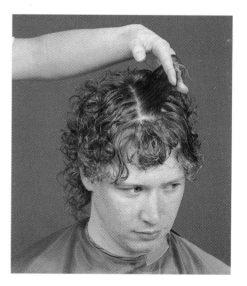

 Bring the hair on each side and in the back up to the center guide and establish a traveling guide as you work over the curve of the head. In the center back just above the occipital bone, begin to bring the hair up to the guide at that position. The hair will begin to get progressively longer from there to maximum length. ⇨

12 The last step is to cut the back to the desired hanging length and balance and blend the layers throughout.

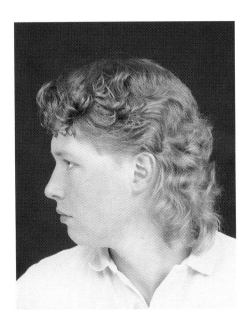

13 The hair may be softly blown into style or allowed to dry naturally for a somewhat curlier look. Either way, the hair should look as if the curl was provided by nature.

Allen

Relaxer

*"While physical
appearance
reveals only a
man's facade,
it also speaks
volumes of his
inner self."*

Darian

M odern, fashion conscious African-American men are prime candidates for multiple grooming services. Most have excessively curly hair that is difficult to control in its natural state. Gone are the days when options for black men were limited to "natural" or narrow structured waves that lay close to the scalp after the hair had been chemically straightened.

Thanks to improved and refined products used to relax or totally remove natural curl and the advanced skills of technicians who specialize in this field, the hair can be "relaxed" and as much or as little curl can be removed to accommodate a variety of fashionable hairstyles.

Darian is a "nouveau" cosmetologist whose talents extend to fashion designing, apparel coordinating, and commentator of fast-moving fashion shows. He knows exactly how he wants to look, the image he wants to project and demands only the best from his stylist.

Essentials

Before

Personal Analysis

After a short conversation with Darian—the technician already knew him—there was little doubt that, in this case, the client would direct the grooming service. At the same time it was evident that he was seeking another's professional opinion. Whether or not he would accept any suggestions probably depended on the way it was presented and the rapport already established.

Technical Analysis

The hair was tightly matted at the scalp and had excessive curl throughout. The hair and scalp were in need of moisturizing. Because the hair was already short, style options were limited. The client had a new growth of facial hair that obviously had not reached its full potential but could be considerably improved with shaping.

Suggested Style

First, at least 50 percent of the curl should be relaxed so it could be styled into a controlled form. Once the curl is removed the hair stretches to a longer length depending on the amount of curl removed, making a haircut necessary. The hair should be cut *after* it is relaxed — not *before*.

Based on the shape of the face, the personality and desires of the client, a closely fitted form with a slight rise at the forehead was suggested.

Procedure

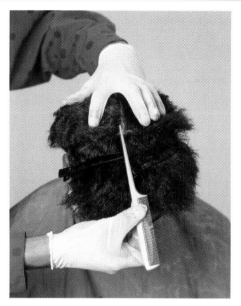

1 The excessively curly hair was without a definite form. The hair on most people's head is not the same texture all over. This client had medium curl in the frontal area and an unmanageable curl in the crown and back areas. The technician-stylist opted to relax only the hair in the back. The degree of relaxation is determined by parting the hair in several places and examining the texture nearest the scalp.

2 Divide the back into two sections — across the crown from ear to ear and from center crown to the nape. Apply a thin coating of petroleum gel to protect the scalp from burns that might occur from harsh chemicals contained in the relaxer product.

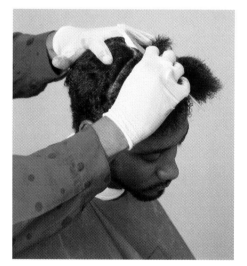

3 Outline the parting with relaxer, keeping the product slightly away from the scalp. The choice of applicators varies from one technician to another. The back of a hard rubber comb or a firm bristle applicator brush works well.

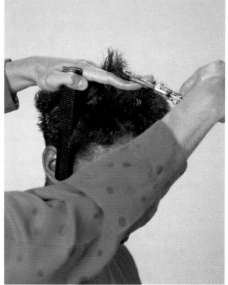

 Make very narrow horizontal partings in each section from the crown to the nape. Apply relaxer to both sides of each panel of hair. On very short hair bring the relaxer product down the entire panel, including the ends, and immediately go back over each section pressing the hair with gloved fingers and the back of a comb until the desired amount of curl is removed.

 Cut the hair beginning in the top center section.

Note *Rinse relaxer from the hair immediately and lather with shampoo prescribed by the manufacturer of the relaxer product used. Repeat the cleansing process until all product is removed from the hair and scalp. Rinse thoroughly and condition as necessary.*

 Establish a length of approximately two and one-half inches in the front angled to about one and one-half inch on the crown and over the curve of the head in the back and on each side.

7 Remove excess length over the entire surface area to create a definite form.

8 Use an adjustable clipper head to feather the edges around the perimeter of the hairline.

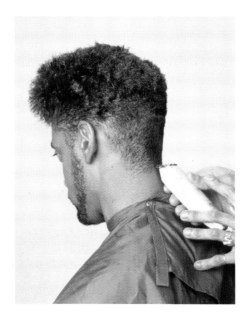

9 Use the finest clipper edge to remove all excess hair from the nape and around the ears. The entire area must be very cleanly clipped or shaven.

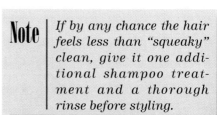

Note | *If by any chance the hair feels less than "squeaky" clean, give it one additional shampoo treatment and a thorough rinse before styling.*

Darian

SPECIALTY TECHNIQUES

Hair Extension

Extending the length of one's natural hair by adding synthetic or real hair wefts is not a new service. It is, however, a highly specialized service.

The techniques used to extend or add volume to existing hair growth is not taught as part of a standard course in cosmetology. There are several highly skilled technicians who specialize in hair weaving and/or bonding that offer classes to licensed cosmetologists or barber-stylists. Their ads can be found in leading trade magazines or in the yellow pages of major cities nationwide.

Like any other technique, hair extension service requires some concentrated training and considerable practice before attempting to service a client.

Fees charged for "hair extension" vary according to how much hair is added. How much you charge for this or any other hair care service depends on many factors. But realistically, it comes down to the cost of time and materials. Of course, you are entitled to some consideration for your unique expertise. It is not a highly competitive field. It is fair to say: "hair extension is a high-ticket service." The rewards are great, both monetarily and for professional prestige.

Most of your hair extension clients will come from "word of mouth" advertising. One satisfied client will tell another. Everyone, at one time or another, has marveled at the magnificent mane displayed by entertainers, most notably Diana Ross and Cher. They have mounds and mounds of beautiful hair that seems to grow overnight. Actually some very talented hairstylist spend hours creating those exotic styles.

Most experts recommend hair pieces (wefts) made of 100 percent human hair that have quality workmanship. Order hair from a company who stands behind the quality of their merchandise. All human hair, before being wefted by the manufacturer, is colored, conditioned, and root-turned. If all hair cuticle is not turned in the same direction as the hair growing on one's head, it will tangle when wet and become impossible to handle. This need not be a concern if you deal with a reputable, well-established manufacturer of hair goods.

The technical vignettes shown in this chapter are meant only to acquaint you with the subject and to pique your interest in learning the art of hair extension.

Specialty Styling

You may have a clientele that has a tendency toward "ethnic" fashion. You may want to pursue such an art—and it is an art. Be aware that it is happening.

There's a universal move toward "show of heritage" fashion, including hairstyles. Men whose roots are buried deep in one of the third-world countries are most likely to reject western styles in favor of their own country's taste. However, the most noticeable are American born men having African ancestry. Many are making bold — and we might say handsome — fashion statements by either twisting or braiding their hair into styles reflecting their heritage.

One such style—dreadlocks—was derived from the style worn by a group in Jamaica, the Rastaferian sect, which was founded in 1930 when Haile Selassie became emperor of Ethiopia.

As a salon professional "awareness" is an important requisite to your financial success. You should be acutely aware of changes in fashion, social tendencies and what influential forces prevail at any given time.

Study trends in hair care carefully so you can be a knowledgeable source of fashion-related information. If you don't wish to diversify your technical skills — many do specialize in one service — at least learn the basics of each current trend.

Dreadlocks styling is big business in some areas. A few salons, located primarily in big cities, specialize in dreadlock innovations in hair. They not only execute the style—which, by the way, is a time consuming and "big-ticket" service—but they retail the products required for maintaining these elaborate creations. Don't be surprised to have Caucasian and non-African–American men with naturally curly hair asking for this service!

If you are not already into specialty styling, it is time to consider broadening your profit margins by adding this rapidly growing source of income.

Hair Replacement

Why even consider a specialty service as demanding as hair replacement?

The reasons vary with each salon professional, but the overriding motive is "extra income." Isn't it time to stop sending your balding clients to technicians who deal exclusively in hair replacement? To date, most salon stylists either refer balding clients to dermatologists who can, and will, prescribe a "hair restorer" product that can only be purchased by a doctor's prescription, or a hair replacement technologist. Neither puts any money in your cash register — and, chances are you just lost a client.

Wouldn't it be great to have a business where you were not constantly replacing the clients who left your salon to try the newest, glitziest salon in the area — clients who have followed one of your employees to a new location?

Because hair replacement is a specialized technique, no course in basic cosmetology prepares you to service these unique clients. There are three kinds of hair replacement services: very good, mediocre, and inadequate. Only the *very good* technician survives today's accelerated competition.

As society places increased value on a youthful, healthy appearance, an increasing number of men — a new generation — are beating a path to the door of hair replacement professionals. Your best prospective clients are apt to be young men who have had no prior experience with "toupees," "rugs," "hairpieces," or "faux" hair. Older men who may have given up on the only hair replacement method available to them, may be hard to reenlist as clients.

Studies compiled by the American Hair Loss Council* show that men are very motivated to do something about their thinning hair. The motivation can be different from age group to age group. While the man in his twenties may want good looking hair to gain the admiration and acceptance of his friends, a man in his thirties may be thinking about the limitations his thinning hair can have on his career ambitions or he may be starting a new social life after a divorce. A man in his forties or fifties may simply want to maximize his appearance to reinforce an image that indicates he has really been successful.

Your knowledge and understanding of the various emotional needs of your prospective hair replacement client can assure your success in this enterprise.

You are in a better position than anyone to advise balding clients when they should consider giving nature a helping hand. Most often the very men who would be the most receptive to that suggestion are the ones who hesitate to broach the subject. In the minds of a sensitive man, replacing his hair closely parallels the panic he'd feel if he was forced suddenly to wear a hearing aid or false teeth. You can put his mind at ease and give him a new lease on life just by making him aware of a few facts about the new technology employed in today's hair replacement systems.

A noted psychologist hired by Upjohn to assist in the marketing plan for the hair growth drug Minoxidil discovered that a man with hair loss problems will consult his hairstylist before his friends, family, or physician. What resulted was the advertising slogan for the tonic Rogaine. "Ask your doctor."

Men are still asking their stylists first. So you are in the enviable position of being able to satisfy his needs and be paid handsomely for doing so.

What Your Potential Clients Should Know About Hair Replacement

The burning question on every potential client's mind is: "Will everyone instantly know that I'm wearing a hair replacement?" The answer, of course, should be a resounding *no*.

The technique and technology used to manufacture today's hair replacement systems far surpasses any method known even a decade ago. As new hair replacements are improved —their appearance is more realistic—old methods simply do not meet the demands of today's discriminating client. It isn't good enough that some hair replacement methods look reasonably natural to the untrained eye. Even under close scrutiny some hair replacement units look quite natural but fail to measure up to the "superbly realistic qualities" of modern hair replacement systems.

Only a hair replacement system of superior quality that has been expertly designed, cut, and styled will appear truly realistic. It should be virtually undetectable even if someone touches the head. It shouldn't matter if it starts to pour rain or the wind whips up to near hurricane velocity. To meet the highest standards a hair replacement system should replicate nature.

A hair replacement should enhance, not diminish the lifestyle of your client. Done correctly it will make the client appear younger and more attractive to himself and others. It is well accepted in today's society that a person is apt to be judged by his appearance. First impressions are still very important. If that impression is unfavorable, it may well be the last meeting. A hair replacement can make a powerful difference in how he is perceived by others.

What Is the Best Method of Hair Replacement

The most common method of covering a balding area is the old-fashioned hair piece or toupee. It has changed little in the last five decades.

They are usually very obvious and have a thick, heavy and sometimes awkward appearance. There's a vast difference between the way a hair piece is made and the technology used in today's refined hair replacement methods. In the old fashioned "piece" as many as eight hairs per knot were used which lends to a heavy, artificial appearance.

Another, rather common method of covering bald areas is called "hair weaving." The name refers basically to a type of attachment. The natural hair left growing on the client's head is tied into a braid or tight cord completely around the balding area. Hair wefts are then stitched to the cord. The natural hair can easily be damaged by the stress put on the hair and scalp—to say nothing of how conspicuous it is to the touch.

Most men will only be interested in a hair replacement method that they perceive to be permanent and not difficult to deal with.

There are several surgical methods for covering bald spots. Only a licensed physician can perform them. While all statistics are far from complete, it is generally thought to be extremely expensive, time consuming and not effective.

The most effective, natural looking and by far the most acceptable replacements are those customized and hand made to individual specifications. Style possibilities are limitless and the replacements are designed to give maximum flexibility.

The best hair replacements are made of virgin human hair, processed human hair and synthetic fiber. The price of each hair replacement is based on the type of hair and the size of the base — the amount of baldness to be covered. Most hair replacement professionals require a 50 percent deposit from the client when the order is placed. The balance to be paid upon delivery.

It isn't difficult to judge a quality hair replacement. Individual hairs appear to sprout from the scalp. These hairs, blended and tied to the replacement's base by craftspersons, mainly in Asia, are hand-tied to a fine screen, polyurethane or a specially designed "integration" structure. Hair tied to a screen mesh will allow for a rotational direction of the hair, while hair tied to polyurethane will impart specific growth angles to the hair.

How to Start

Contact the best manufacturer of hair products you can find. Attend technical classes to learn all aspects of color matching, measuring, fitting, and attaching by more than one method.

You already know how to cut and style the hair of your male clients, but you will need to learn all the unique cutting techniques required for a hair replacement. Consider joining an organization such as the American Hair Loss Council to stay abreast of new techniques, products, and hair replacement sources.

Analyze the space you have available. Find an area with maximum privacy. Hair replacement is one service that men take very seriously. To them it is a private matter — not to be shared with anyone — much less a salon full of "strangers." You might even consider a private entrance. If that is not possible consider a partition with an impressive masculine doorway. Just inside the private area make a small waiting area. Provide reading material of interest to men only — Golf Digest, Car & Driver, Playboy, etc. Take a note from smart medical professionals and run a video of a great hair replacement procedure. It's sure to get their attention!

Do not make your prospect walk past rows of hair dryers or women in rollers to get to his consultation. He is usually quite embarrassed to be discussing this personal problem, particularly with a stranger.

Finally, don't be cavalier with these clients. Be courteous, friendly, empathetic, and above all professional. You are his closest confidant at this meeting, sharing a personal secret that even his closest friends don't know about.

It is well to remember that many of your potential hair replacement clients have been referred to you by other satisfied clients. There's an old adage that rings true, "A satisfied client will tell ten others, a dissatisfied client will tell a hundred!"

*Special thanks to the American Hair Loss Council for providing a reliable source of information for this book.

The American Hair Loss Council provides information to salon professionals on request. You may write to:

AMERICAN HAIR LOSS COUNCIL

100 Independence Place, Suite 207
Tyler, TX 75703
or you may call 1-800-274-8717

Weaving

"To men who traditionally wear short hair, very long hair often represents a unique luxury."

Robbie

L et's face it! Every man that walks through your salon door will *not* be asking for "longer" hair. There are those who will ask, and you or a member of your designer staff should be prepared. By any method, hair extension is a salon specialty. If only one employee in each salon is an expert in this field, it will allow a very "high ticket service" to be offered.

Extending the length of hair by the "weaving" method is highly technical and you should seek hands-on practice with someone experienced in the art of "weave extension" before trying it on a client.

Robbie's physical appearance is directly related to his personal taste. His long hair does not reveal his occupation. He is project manager for a placement company engaged in what is commonly referred to as "head hunting." His company seeks out and finds positions for highly skilled technicians and administrators to fill specialized, high-salaried positions.

Because he does not deal in person with the client or the potential employee, he needn't fit any corporate dress code. He is in an enviable position.

Essentials

Before

Personal Analysis

When a client comes to designer-technician, Michael Wade, there is little doubt how he wants his hair styled. Michael has a sizeable following. Men and women seek his extension services. His reputation is exemplary and most clients are recommended by other satisfied clients. This client is a young, gifted businessman who enjoys wearing his hair long, in a loose ponytail or a controlled braid. His taste in music includes classical and progressive jazz. His hobbies are all people oriented.

Technical Analysis

Long hair is nothing new to this client. A month ago his own hair was well below shoulder length. A friend gave him a trim, much shorter than expected. He wants it long again and hasn't the patience to wait for it to grow at the rate of one-half inch a month. The natural hair is in good condition. The natural color is almost black.

Suggested Style

The designer-technician met with Robbie three weeks prior to the actual extension service. A sample of the natural hair was "snipped" so the color could be matched perfectly with the weft of hair necessary for extension. At that time the length of the extension was also discussed. The stylist recommended a length not to exceed his former natural growth. Because wefts come pre-waved or straight, Robbie's natural texture was carefully noted. While hair extensions can be shampooed like the hair that grows on the head a regular regimen of professional treatments is recommended. Some balsam conditioners may result in a coating that is not easily removed from weft extensions.

Procedure

Note | *The client wanted his hair restored to its original length before a less than pleasing hair trim.*

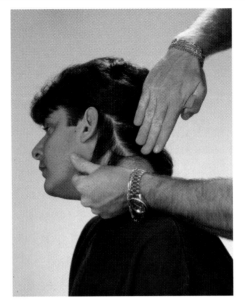

1 Part off a two inch section behind each ear. The braid to which the weft will be attached must start at least two inches from the hairline so it cannot be detected when the hair is pulled away from the face.

2 Make a horizontal part about two inches above the natural hair growth at the nape. Clip all the hair up and out of the way. Execute a very narrow braid either a French braid or Corn row, from behind each ear to center back allowing the prescribed distance away from each ear. Thread a curved carpet needle with heavy-duty thread and begin to secure the braids together.

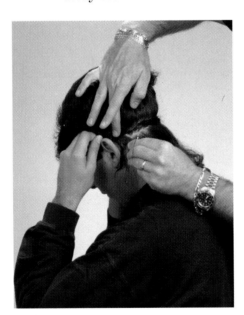

3 Keep the curve (not the point) of the needle near the scalp and make an over and under stitch. Follow with a loop in the opposite direction and under the initial stitches.

4 When the thread is cut, tie it several times and leave a four inch lead just to be sure it does not slip from the knot.

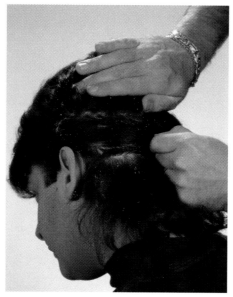

5 When the first braid is secured repeat the braiding and sewing procedure two to three inches above the original braid, just under the occipital bone.

6 Hold the weft of hair across the head, the distance of the braid, and cut to the exact length

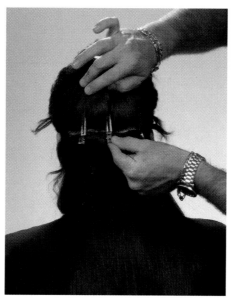

7 Use clips to hold the weft in place over the lower braid and repeat the same stitching procedure to attach the weft securely to the braid.

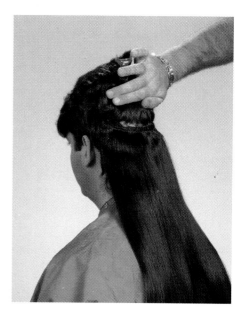

8 Repeat the entire weft attachment procedure on the top braid. ⇨

 Brush the natural hair down over the weft extensions and carefully blend the sides to a natural looking flow.

 Use a rotating comb-over-razor technique to scatter the surface lengths and blend the natural hair with the new wefted extension.

Note *The weave method of adding length to natural hair is practical inasmuch as it can easily be removed and rewoven as the hair grows and the braids loosen from the scalp. Removal of the wefts will not damage the natural hair in any way and can be treated as natural hair growth as long as it is in place.*

Robbie

Bonding

*"Public performers
have a tendency
to create an image
to impress an
audience."*

Kevin

Hair extension can often be the solution to a mistake made by one or more "less than perfect" haircuts.

Kevin tediously grew his hair to one length all over. It hung just below the shoulders and could easily be pulled away from the face or left "flowing" on special occasions. The hair has a great natural curl but could not be shown off to advantage when the front hair was as long as the back.

He asked a barber-stylist to cut his hair on the top to a more manageable length and to undercut the nape area and sideburns. Mistakenly, the hair was cut short on the sides as well, leaving length only in the back. When the hair was pulled back in a pony tail or braid, the sides looked bare. He began looking for someone to repair the damage, and he was referred to Craig Wilson, a specialist in hair bonding. In fact, the device used in this step-by-step technical was designed by Craig. He has a patent pending.

In order to consider your establishment a "full service" salon, you should have technical and practical skills in every service required to accommodate the needs of a variety of clients. Adding length or volume to hair by "bonding" is a valuable and profitable service.

Essentials

Before

Personal Analysis

Kevin is already an accomplished pianist but hardly considers his musical education complete. While still in college, studying music, he gains experience by playing either alone or with a group at clubs, cocktail lounges, or at special presentations. He is unpretentious and totally unaffected by his acclaimed success, even at this early age. He definitely wants his appearance to reflect his attitude and embraces the idea that long hair enhances his artistic image.

Technical Analysis

The extreme ends of the hair are quite dry and show evidence of breakage. Most men are inclined to abuse long hair by letting it "twist in the wind" or by incorrect brushing. The short areas are in good condition. The natural haircolor is medium warm brown, level 6. The big problem seems to be lack of length on the sides.

Suggested Style

Additional hair is needed on the sides only in the temple area. Hair extension by the weave method could not be done because the hair is too short for the strip-braiding necessary to attach a hair weft. Even if the hair was longer a weave is not easy to camouflage in that area. So hair extension by a bonding method was recommended. To give the hair a little interest in the front a slight bit of bleach was brushed onto the surface and left only until the hair lifted one level. Then it was removed.

Procedure

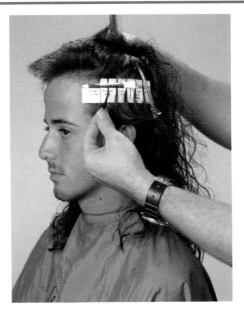

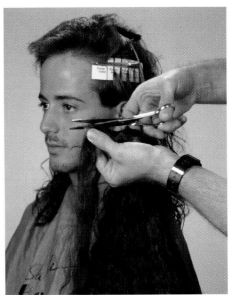

1 Part the hair on one side in preparation for bonding hair extensions to the natural short hair growth. Use a paper-cardboard ruler. Cut slots one inch apart across a length extending from the hairline to a point just back of the ear and pull a "pea size" strand of hair through each slot.

2 Cut a piece of hair from a color matched weft the same diameter as that pulled through the slot. The length of the hair weft must match the length of the natural hair in the back.

3 Squeeze a drop of hair bonding glue onto the end of the extension that is to be attached to the natural hair.

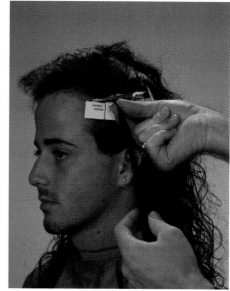

 Apply bonding glue to the natural hair at the exact point the extension will be attached.

 Overlap the extension approximately one-half inch onto the natural hair, hold the two pieces together until they are firmly fused together.

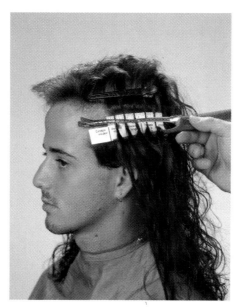

 Repeat the same bonding procedure across the entire slotted device. Then make one or more strips of attachments keeping each about two inches apart.

 Comb the integrated hair down to remove any snarls.

8 Use a razor to create subtle surface layers to more closely match the natural hair growth in the back. Carefully blend the hair extensions with the natural hair. No difference in texture should be visible.

Note *The hair extensions can easily be removed by reheating the glue connection and simply pulling the extension away from the natural hair.*

Kevin

Dreadlocks

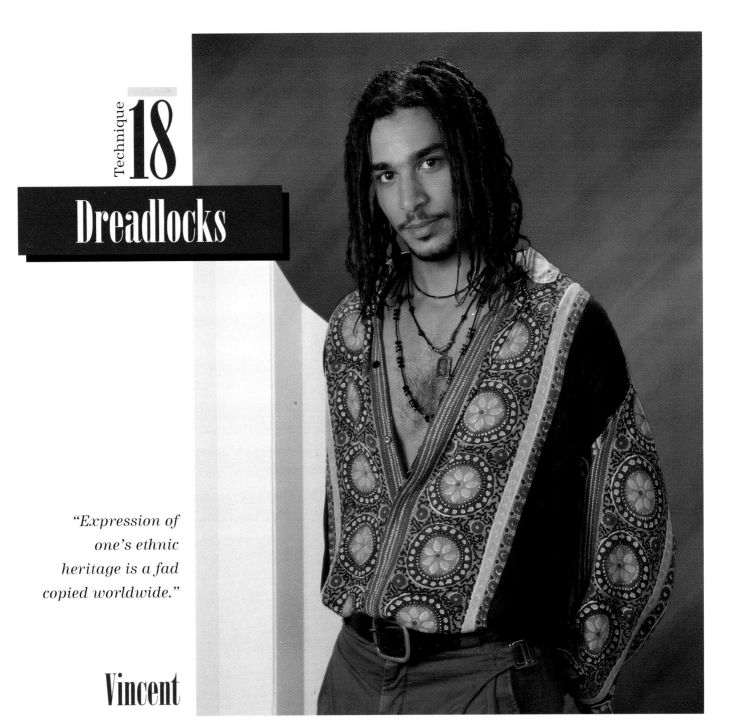

"Expression of one's ethnic heritage is a fad copied worldwide."

Vincent

There are a growing number of young adults, especially of ethnic nationality, that seek out visible ways of identifying with their own heritage. Some are even engaged in the entertainment field or excel in creative crafts.

Limited research suggests these highly motivated individuals most often patronize professional salons that specialize in the skills necessary to design and execute the "fad" hairstyles they demand. Black hair care is a spe-

cialized art, and requires additional training in order to master the skills necessary to attract and hold a clientele. You need to gain the confidence of only a few Black clients. The clients will multiply by favorable recommendation.

Vincent is a multifaceted artist capable of choosing many avenues of earning money and satisfying his artistic tendencies. He holds a cosmetology license, plies his hair design skills in an upscale salon located in a prestigious and wealthy neighborhood, and clings to his love of music — specifically Reggae. His clay sculptures, featuring primitive tribal dancers, are sought-after collectors items.

Essentials

Personal Analysis

This is a man who leaves no doubt about his tastes in hairstyles. He chooses his hairstyle to complement his total look. He has the technical skill to do his own hair, but like many people lacks the time and desire to do so.

Technical Analysis

The hair is not black, but a rich dark brown, level 2. It is in good condition despite its length. Because dreadlocks are more easily formed in "natural" hair having no chemical treatment, there is no chemical damage present. There's no way to remove "dreadlocks" other than cutting the hair. Vincent is well aware of this. His intention is to keep this look as long as it suits his personal preference, then move on to some other equally self-expressive style.

Suggested Style

The style is "cast in stone," but the client is advised to get the ends of the hair trimmed regularly and each time the hair needs re-twisting. It should have a deep moisturizing treatment under light steam. This will prevent the hair from becoming brittle. Vincent enhances his Reggae appearance with a narrow mustache and a shadow Van Dyke beard. Facial hair needs professional shaping as well.

Procedure

Dreadlocks is a word that describes a head full of strands of hair twisted into tight rope like formations.

The size of the twisted strands depends largely on the length and thickness of the hair. Hair crafters who specialize in the art of "dreadlocks" identify strand sizes as "peewee," "small", "medium," and "large."

Use a water soluble oil, preferably containing a nutrient such as aloe vera. Rub a small amount into the palm of your hands and onto your fingers. As you twist each strand oil each well enough to control stray hairs and contribute to manageability.

Start twisting, or retwisting, the hair at the perimeter and work toward the crown and finally to the face frame. Each finished strand will overlay the one underneath. A controlled procedure of twisting speeds the process and protects the finished "locks" as other strands are twisted.

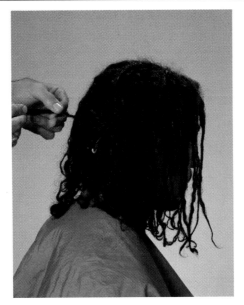

1 Start twisting each hair strand as close to the scalp as possible. The direction in which the strand is twisted is irrelevant unless you wish to create a particular pattern, for example, away from the face or a mushroom crown.

2 Continue to twist the strand from scalp to end maintaining tension throughout.

Note *To keep their dreadlocks in best condition clients should be advised to have the hair retwisted every 3-4 weeks. In-salon dry shampoo treatments and regular conditioning will keep the hair soft, shiny and natural looking. It is important to regularly trim "raggedy" ends as the hair grows.*

Vincent

Removable System

"What nature fails to provide modern technology replicates."

John

Men who are losing, or have lost all or any part of their natural hair, cannot be classified together. It can happen to anyone, young or old, rich or poor, or in any walk of life.

Most men do not handle "balding" very graciously. Their first reaction ranges from denial to a near nervous breakdown. It is fair to say few just shrug it off.

Men whose careers depend, to some degree, on physical appearance are the most aggressive in seeking the best hair replacement service available. However, many men with jobs or professions where hair is no particular asset can be near panic at the slightest notice of hair loss.

When dealing with the needs of a client with any degree of hair loss several considerations are imperative. First, you must realize how vulnerable this man feels. You must recognize that even the slightest amount of hair loss can concern some men. It is not uncommon for a man to purchase a hair replacement to cover hair that he considers unsightly. But, most men are interested in the most advanced hair replacement method, *not* what he perceives to be a hairpiece.

Your discussion with him should include technical descriptions and language. You should avoid any slang terms. Cosmetic dentists today talk about "bonded teeth" or "implants," never "caps" or "false teeth." Likewise your terminology should be equally professional yet graphic.

A man will pay a considerable sum for a "high-quality hair replacement system bonded to, and integrated with, his own growing hair," but he isn't going to want to spend much for "a piece of hair glued to his head."

Because the product and service you are selling needs maintenance and eventually wears out, you must be forthright in discussing its care and the inevitable repurchase plan. Some men can well afford the initial cost of a replacement but may balk at the ongoing costs if not correctly presented.

Remember, most men are not accustomed to spending a lot of money on their hair, as many women do routinely. However they will do so gladly when they realize the benefits.

Some clients simply have no knack for styling their own hair, much less the skill to handle additional hair. Hair replacement experts agree that there is no way to know in advance who will have an easy time of it. The best approach is an honest and thorough presenta-tion, emphasizing the positive experience of your happy clients.

Many of his fears will be dispelled as he gains confidence in your ability as an accomplished and well-informed technician. Overcoming these obstacles is prerequisite to the successful sale of a hair replacement. This can only be accomplished through knowledge. If you are seriously considering hair replacement as a major salon service, you and your staff must take advantage of education offered by different hair loss organizations, manufacturers and technicians recognized as expert in the field.

Information pertaining to hair loss and hair replacement service contained in the introduction of this text was carefully gathered from successful professionals in this highly specialized field.

John, the model in this technical, owns a very successful hair replacement business with locations in the United States and Europe. As you might imagine, his own hair loss made him acutely aware of the needs of other balding men. He counsels his clients with sensitivity, empathy and a vast amount of knowledge augmented by personal experience. His technical knowledge of every aspect of hair replacement makes him one of the best known and most respected in the business.

Essentials

Personal Analysis

Before

This client, while a great deal more knowledgeable than most of your balding clients, still typifies the basic attitude of a man who has decided to make a serious decision about his personal appearance. Some men will be deeply interested in every aspect of this new adventure while others just want you to give them "great hair." Hair replacement candidates will undoubtedly ask more questions about the commitment they are considering than clients considering chemical services.

He realizes it is a long-term commitment. His satisfaction depends greatly on his willingness to maintain the replacement unit on a daily basis. He knows as well that follow-up visits to a professional hair replacement specialist are vital to the success of this venture. He understands from in-depth conversation with the technician that he is not buying an article to be worn once in awhile. He is happily and willingly making an investment in his physical appearance and his emotional stability.

Note: Most of your potential clients know very little about hair replacement. Many have been disappointed or misinformed in the past. The initial sale and ultimate client satisfaction will depend on your presentation.

Technical Analysis

This is a clear case of male pattern baldness in its most extreme form. All hair on top of the head and well over the natural curve in the crown is missing. The scalp is totally bare of all but a few wispy strands, making integration impossible.

There is natural hair growth quite high on either side of the head that could be used for bonding if that was a selective service. The existing hair growth is quite dense and the texture tends to have a natural wave movement. The natural color is salt and pepper. There is about 50 percent gray mixed with a cool dark brown, level 5. Each of those factors—density, texture, and color—are major considerations when ordering a custom made hair replacement.

Suggestion

There is no doubt that a standard hair replacement unit, covering the entire balding area, one that can easily be removed and replaced on a daily or weekly basis will be the logical recommendation of the stylist-technician. The client will feel less pressure learning how to handle a hair replacement unit that can, with little effort, be removed and reapplied as he chooses. The client agrees.

Preparation

The technically minded client wants nothing left to the imagination.

He wants to be told:

1. *The kind of hair replacement being ordered*
   a) its quality
   b) its structure

2. *The approximate time of delivery*
   An appointment should be made for fitting after delivery and the initial styling

3. *The price of the replacement.*
   The price should be discussed prior to this time but be sure you restate the total price including fitting and styling.

4. *Some explanation of the long-term cost*
   This must be addressed, keeping in mind that the product will wear out in time and need to be replaced.

Procedure

Measuring

1 Use the texture shears to snip a sizeable lock from the client's natural hair.

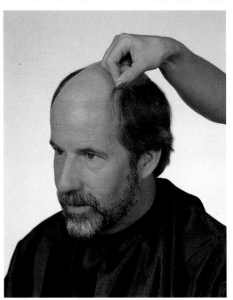

2 Take the sample from an area that matches the hair growing nearest his face as closely as possible. If the natural hair color varies greatly from front to back take a sampling from the back area as well. When the hair replacement unit is custom made you can request more or less gray in specific areas of the head.

3 Pull a piece of plastic wrap over the bald area. Take particular care to cover the front hair line. Place a template at center forehead exactly where the natural hairline would occur and use a wide marker to outline the template.

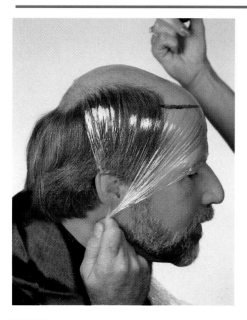

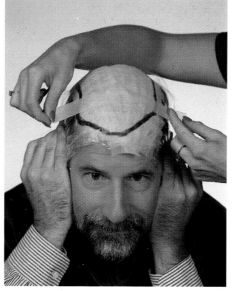

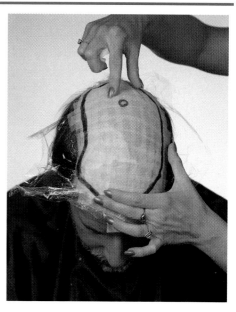

4 Continue to outline the bald area. Mark just below the natural hair growth on each side to center crown. If necessary add a second piece of plastic wrap overlapping the one used for outlining the front (not shown) and mark completely around the balding area in the back.

5 Cover the entire outlined area using cellophane tape. A precise fitting of the polyurethane base is extremely important. First lay tape from side to side then reinforce the area by criss-crossing the tape from front to back.

6 Make a small circle at the spot where a strong directional hair growth might naturally occur.

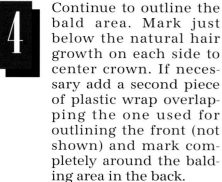

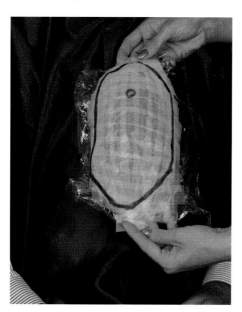

7 Remove the pattern in one piece and examine it carefully for precise measurements. This pattern along with hair samples will be sent to the custom manufacturer for the finest hair replacement system available.

Note *The replacement unit is made of human hair with the exception of the percentage of gray, which is a fine quality fiber. This mixture enables the technician to refresh the hair color as it fades from the sun and constant shampooing. The human hair will accept hair color, the synthetic fibers will not. With proper grooming products and regular service visits, the replacement will remain as fresh looking as the day it was delivered.*

Fitting after Delivery

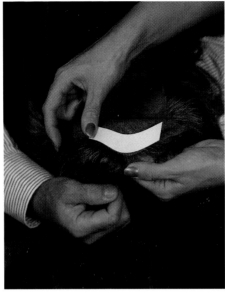

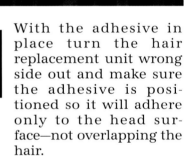

 Place medical grade double sided, non allergenic adhesive strips around the perimeter of the hair replacement base. Adhesive made specifically for this purpose is preshaped to fit closely around the curved perimeter.

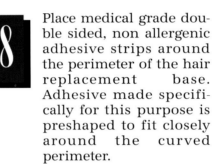 With the adhesive in place turn the hair replacement unit wrong side out and make sure the adhesive is positioned so it will adhere only to the head surface—not overlapping the hair.

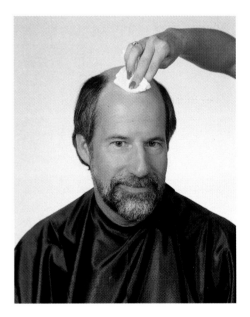

 Thoroughly cleanse the scalp with alcohol. Apply a medical skin prep to create a dry film barrier between the scalp and the polyurethane base of the hair replacement unit.

 Pull the outside protective cover from the adhesive, exposing the transparent fixative interior.

Start at the front hairline and roll the hair replacement onto the scalp firmly pressing it into place. ⇨

The Shaping

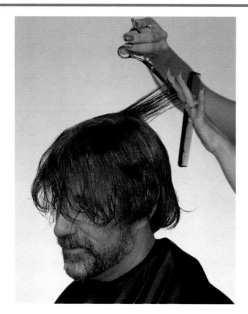

13 When cutting a hair piece use a slither stroke and cut from the top towards the perimeter to effect a perfect blend with the natural hair growth.

14 When the perimeter length and blend has been established cut the crown to a length coinciding with the first traveling guide. Cut the hair as precisely as possible keeping in mind the replacement hair will not grow but the natural hair will. The replacement perimeter length should be cut to a length that allows for at least a half-inch growth between visits to the salon.

15 The last step is to create baby fine hair resembling natural hairline growth all around the forehead. Unless this is skillfully done the frontal hairline will appear blunt to close inspection — the last thing the client or the technician wants to happen.

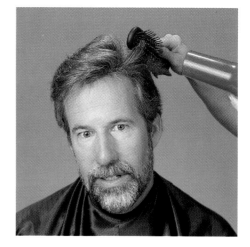

16 Dampen the hair using a fine mist spray bottle and blow it into style. Voila, miraculous reconstruction emulating nature!

John

Technique 20
Integrated System

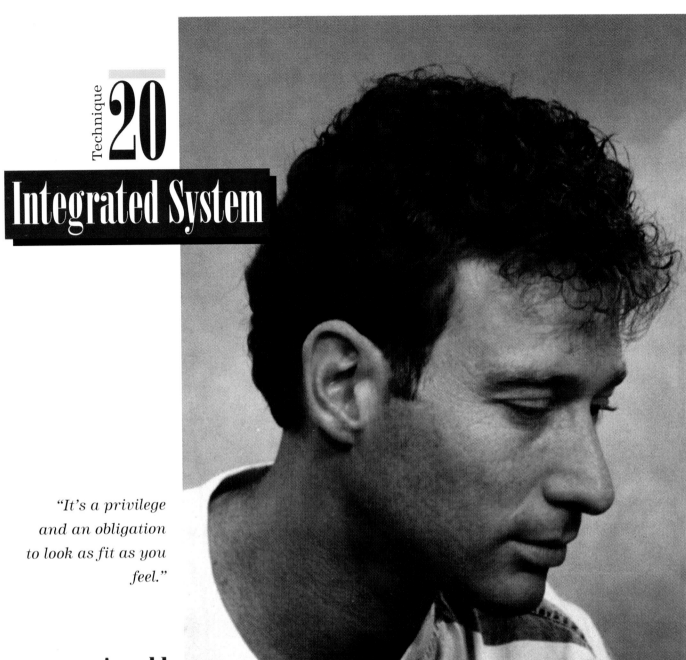

"It's a privilege and an obligation to look as fit as you feel."

Arnold

Not every man waits until he is totally bald to look for ways to either restore or replace lost hair. While it's a relatively new practice for women to shampoo their hair on a daily basis, men have been doing so for as long as most of them can remember. A man virtually inventories each hair every day. He knows, almost to the hour, when it starts to thin. Contrary to the facade most men present, they are deeply concerned.

Only in the last decade have choices been made available to balding men. Once they could either join the "bald is beautiful" brigade; disguise it with the laughable "comb-over"; or wear what was commonly called a toupee or hair piece. The latter seemed repulsive so the result was to let nature take its course.

Now there's a hair replacement system for men —and women as well—that is so subtle, effective, undetectable, and outright comfortable that no one needs to suffer through gradual hair loss.

That system is known as the hair integration system. It quite literally adds hair to that still growing on the scalp, then integrates the two to look and feel like one healthy growth of natural hair.

Arnold Daniels has a Ph.D. in electrical engineering. He has earned the title of Dr. Daniels. He is actively involved in research in electro-optics and laser test systems for infrared modifications for maximum effectiveness in many areas, including use in nighttime combat.

Essentials

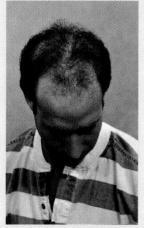

Before

(Two views) There is sufficient hair growing on the head to effectively use an integrated hair replacement system.

Personal Analysis

Dr. Daniels is no lightweight. However, he is not a gregarious man. He volunteers very little about his personal likes and dislikes. Even in casual conversation, his unwillingness to accept hair loss is obvious. He blames many hours of intense study, stress and frustration for the early onslaught of male pattern baldness. He is a relatively young man with a brilliant future and is totally unwilling to accept hair loss as inevitable.

Once he was told of the hair integration system whereby new hair could be integrated with his own, he was ready for action!

Technical Analysis

The hair on top has been reduced through progressive hair loss to about 40 percent of its natural growth potential. The average density in that area is approximately 800 hairs per square inch. The appearance changes with the size of each hair, i.e., fine, medium fine, or coarse. Dr. Daniel's natural hair is medium fine. In addition, he has a tendency toward a receding hairline which is now exaggerated due to the extent of hair loss. The color of his natural hair is light reddish brown, a color usually associated with natural red heads. A few freckles and "boyish" features further support that observation.

Suggestions

The integrated hair replacement system is a natural for this client. The important things to consider when custom ordering this system are:

1. the color of the existing hair

2. its density and texture

3. the amount of hair needed to complete a full head of hair, i.e., the openings in the base of the replacement system which allow natural hair to grow through.

What the Client Should Know

The client must be told that the hair in the replacement system will require a color treatment from time to time. It will gradually fade from regular shampooing and sun exposure. The color is easily restored because it is made entirely of human hair that can be tinted to a perfect match.

Inasmuch as the natural hair grows approximately one-half inch a month, the system must be removed and rebonded every 4–6 weeks. Skilled technicians can remove a system, renew and refresh the color, cut the client's hair, and replace the system in less than an hour. The client should know exactly how much time and money he is investing.

Prices of the initial system vary, but a custom made integrated human hair system is usually priced between 500 and 1,500 dollars. Servicing fees vary from one area to another — and from one studio to another — but a potential client can expect maintenance costs of 35 to 60 dollars each time the system is serviced or the natural hair is shaped or the color renewed.

In addition, the client must know up front that hair replacement systems do not last forever. They will wear out sooner or later and need to be replaced. Good professional service will preserve the system for a long time, but don't mislead the client into believing it will last for a lifetime.

Preparation

The technique for measuring the bald area to be covered does not vary. Different measuring techniques are used. It is prudent to create a plaster mold for each client with all pertinent information and measurements inscribed on the mold. Each individual mold is labeled and becomes a permanent file. In time the mold may have to be redone as the bald area increases or the natural hair becomes even more sparse.

Procedure

Fitting

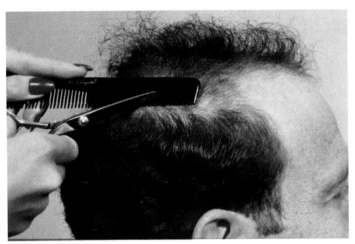

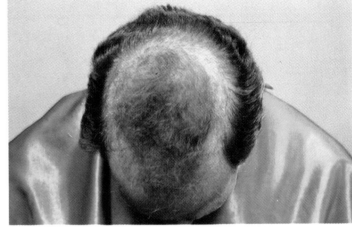

 1 After the hair and scalp have been thoroughly cleansed cut a channel (path) completely around the perimeter of the hair loss area. The channel should be approximately one-half inch to three-quarter inches wide, the actual width of the perimeter binding on the hair system. Leave about a quarter-inch of stubble. A scissor-over-comb technique is most effective for this procedure.

 2 A view of the completed channel.

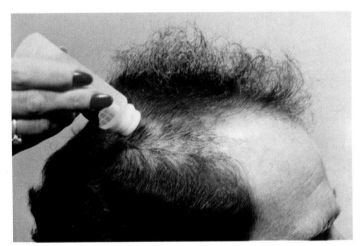

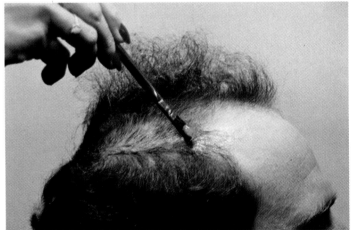

 3 Apply medical prep to form a dry protective barrier between the skin and the system's adhesive binding.

 4 Apply medical adhesive to the hair stubble. The adhesive will bond to the prep, not to the scalp.

 Now apply medical adhesive to the system's perimeter binding. Place a "removable" adhesive strip at the center forehead.

Note *The adhesive strip at center forehead must be removed and replaced by the client between salon visits. The strip may be removed every day, but under no circumstance should it be left on longer than a week*

6 Start at the front hairline and press the perimeter of the system to the matching channel.

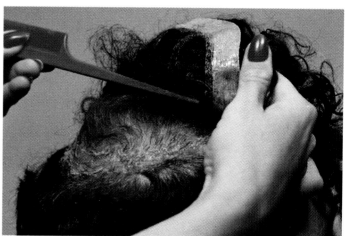

 As the two surfaces make contact be sure to push all the natural hair up and under so it can be pulled through the openings ⇨

 Use the end of a rat-tailed comb to press the system firmly into place. The bond is quick and strong and can only be removed by a technician at the time of servicing. No normal activity will dislodge the system once it is properly applied.

 Start at the back of the system and progressively pull all the natural hair through the openings

The Shaping

 Blend the sides and back and create an adaptable form.

 Cut the face-frame last. Use a slithering technique throughout, but especially in the frontal area. The hair should be made to look exactly like his natural hair growth.

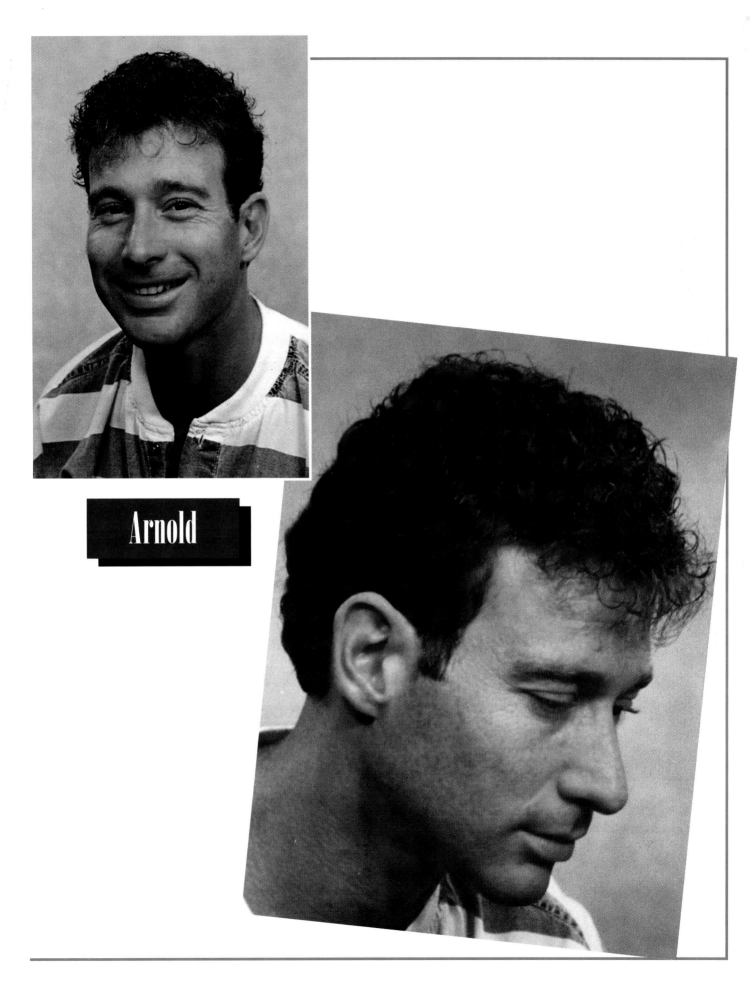

Arnold

Glossary

A

abnormalities: quality or condition of being less normal; irregularities

accurate: state of being exact, free from error

acquired: modification of structure or function gained by one's own effort, generally regarded as not inherited

acumen: sharp insight

adaptable: ability to change without difficulty to conform to surrounding circumstances

adhere: to stick fast; allegiance and support to one's own belief

adhesive: strip of fabric having a sticky substance on one side

African-American: person born in America, having African ancestry

aggressive: bold and energetic in pursuit of one's goals

alcohol: any of a series of compounds made of grain; ethyl or ethanol for use as disinfectant; intoxicating ingredient or fuel

altering: to change or modify

ample: sufficient in size or scope; more than enough to determine one's nature or tendencies

angular: having sharply defined angles; prominent bones forming facial features

artificial: made in imitation of nature

asymmetrical: not symmetrical; an object having dimensions not identical on both sides

attachment: anything that attaches a thing or person to another; devoted to an object, person or idea

avant garde: advance guard; out in front; ahead

B

balding: gradual loss of hair on the head

balsam: oily, gummy, aromatic resin obtained from certain trees and plants, used in some hair conditioners

barber-stylist: person licensed in the skills of "barbering-styling" and "cosmetology"

base: point of attachment; the foundation or most important element

blend: to mix or merge units so there is no noticeable demarcation

blow dryer: hand-held instrument for drying hair by the force of air

blunt: having a straight, unbeveled edge

bold: daring; free in behavior or manner

bonding: holding units together using any adhesive substance

buzz: a slang word for cutting the hair very short using clippers

C

camouflage: to disguise or make less obvious

casual: informal; careless disregard; a title given sportswear apparel

caucasian: member of the caucasian race, loosely refers to a "white" person

cavalier: treated lightly; arrogant; insensitive attitude

charismatic: special quality of leadership; having a pleasing, magnetic personality

chemically relaxed: hair that has some or all of the curl removed by the use of a chemical usually sodium hydroxide or ammonium thyoclycolic acid

classic: generally recognized and accepted as excellent; simple, balanced, formal art forms

clipper: a barber's tool used for cutting hair

clipper head: clipper attachment used to automatically adjust the length of hair left on the head

clipper-over-comb: cutting hair by placing a comb between the scalp and the clipper head

coating: covering the surface without penetration

coincide: the same in shape, position and area

color lifting: removing all or part of the natural color from the hair

complementary: that which completes or brings to perfection

complete: finished; accomplished

compromised: adjustment of opposing principals or ideas by which part of each is given up

conform: to be in accord or agreement; to be or become similar

conservative: tendency to preserve established tradition

contemporary: living or happening in the same period of time

contour: outline of a figure, object, or mass

corn row: term used for braiding the hair close to the scalp in narrow rows

cotton strip: rolled strip of cotton used primarily to protect the facial area from chemical drip

cross-cutting: cutting the hair in the opposite directions for a refined finish and accuracy

curved: all or any part of a circular pattern

curved needle: large curved needle used for flat, inflexible surfaces, most notably, carpets; adapted for use in attaching hair wefts

cuticle: outer layer of the skin; protective scale of the surface of each hair strand

D

damp: some moisture is retained

define: to determine or set boundaries; to explain the meaning

density: thickness

design clipper: cutting instrument for detailing thickness

detailing: accessorizing, finishing touches

developer: chemical used to activate bleach or tint

diagonal: slanting between two opposite corners; often referring to a 45 degree angle

diffuser: device attached to a hand held hair dryer to muffle or reduce the air flow

dimensional: having a specified number of dimensions, i:.e., width, length, and height

diminish: reduce; make smaller

direct: straightforward; straight; not deviating

discretionary: at once's own discretion, individual choice

discriminating: to be selective

dispelled: dispensed with; put aside

dreadlocks: name given to a hairstyle created by followers of Haile Selassie

E

egotistical: self-centered

elevate: to lift up

elongate: to lengthen; to make longer than wide

empathize: to participate in the feelings or ideas of another

emulate: trying to equal; replicate

enhancer: capability of making greater; intensifier

entrepreneur: person who assumes risk for high profit stakes

excessive: curl more curl than can be easily controlled

excessively: far beyond what is usual or average

extension: addition; to widen, lengthen or expand

exudes: ooze; obvious outpouring

F

facial features: form and structure of the face; facial appearance

faux: manmade; not a product of nature

feathering: lightly removing weight and scattering lengths at the end of hair strands

fine tooth: special comb often used for shingling, having very closely fitted teeth

finishing lotion: liquid product used for controlling hair as the style is being detailed

firmly: held with strength; tightly

flat-top: haircut, so named because the top is flat as opposed to following the shape of the head

flattering: making one look his very best

form: the shape or outline of anything

forty-five degrees: diagonal line; half of a right angle

french braid: three strand braid working each strand on the scalp as opposed to progressing down the hair strand

G

glue: dispenser container for applying glue

glue gun: tool in which glue pellets are inserted and melted to application consistency

glue pellets: glue sticks in solid form for specific use in glue guns or glue applicators

gradually: a little at a time

growth pattern: natural hair growth and direction

guide: measured length from which to judge surrounding or blended lengths

H

hair loss: term used when natural hair falls from its follicle

hair replacement: term used to indicate professional technique for replacing natural hair by supplementing or replacing one's real hair with manmade hair systems

hair restorers: products applied to the scalp in an effort to stimulate hair growth

hairline: line at which the hair begins to grow around the face frame, nape, and over the ears

harmony: complementary one to another; well suited; complete blend

highlights: portion of one's natural haircolor made slightly lighter for light reflection or interest

horizontal: parallel to the plane of the horizon; as opposed to vertical

horseshoe parting: half circle part in the crown of the head used for creating a hair cut

I

incision: to cut into

increase: make larger, longer or wider

indigenous: native to a region; inherent

initial: first; the beginning

integration: mixed together; to bring parts together as a whole

irregular: uneven

irregularities: out of range of normality; abnormalities

J

jock: slang word used to describe a man whose hobbies and lifestyle are absorbed by sports

K

knowledgeable: well informed; educated; having correct information

L

layered: various lengths throughout; as opposed to one overall length

level: scale of values; hair color is measured at levels 1–10, 1 being the darkest

lift capability: term used to describe how much natural color can be removed from the hair by one specific product

lifter: object used to lightly lift and separate hair strands

low-light: term used when strands of hair are made darker than the mass

M

mainstream: following acceptable standards

male-pattern baldness: the loss of one's hair in the center crown

manageable: flexible; can be made to conform

maximum: the peak; the most

minimum: the least amount

modern: current

N

nape: the hairline at the back of the neck

napped: wool-like hair adhered to the scalp

natural fall: the way the hair hangs naturally

new breed: slang expression meaning a member of the young progressive generation

no blend: more than one form in the same hair cut

nonporous: solid; cannot be penetrated by moisture

nouveau: new; now

O

oblong: long oval

obstacles: anything that gets in the way or hinders

occipital: bone a bone in the back of the head at the base of the skull

on-base: positioned directly in the center of a sectioned space

original: guide the length first established

outline: the form

over-directed: a section of hair wrapped in a perm rod and positioned above its base

P

panels: vertical partings

parallel: on the same plane peaked maximum; reaching a high point

perimeter: around the outside

peroxide: H_2O_2; a developer used to chemically activate bleach and tint

plastic cap: similar to a shower cap used in processing some chemical hair services

plastic picks: small stick, having pointed ends, made of plastic or nonporous material

pocket: having three to four secured sides, capable of holding material

polyurethane: a synthetic rubber polymer

pompadour: hair raised at the forehead

ponytail: hair pulled away from the face and secured at the center back and resembling a pony's tail

practical: a realistic approach; concerned with or dealing efficiently with every day activities

pre-cut: having been previously cut

precise: exact; explicit

preppies: a word given to a conservative youth group in the fifties.

prime: the first in quality; excellence; the best part of anything

priority: first in order of importance

professional: licensed; acknowledged expert in his field of endeavor

progressive: moving forward or onward

proportioned: the comparative relation between parts

prudent: cautious; capable of exercising sound judgement

R

rapport: agreeable relationship

razor: sharp edged cutting instrument

realistic: practical rather than visionary replicate to copy an original

reality: the real thing, as opposed to fantasy

reattach: to connect something once severed

receded: moved back from original growth

receding: to move back

recluse: to live apart from others; solitary

reconstruction: rebuild; to make over

reduce: to make smaller; less

refine: to make better; free from imperfection

reflect: light returned from a surface

regimen: regular routine

relax: to release strictness

relaxed: made less structured

relaxer: chemical product that softens the hair making excess curl relax into a wider wave pattern

reluctant: less than eager; hesitant

repeat: to do the same thing over

replacement: person or thing that takes the place of another

respond: to act in return

restructured: to change the natural shape or form

rope-like: resembling the appearance of a rope

round brush: hair brush having bristles circling a round base

rounding: having no square corners

rubber base: hair brush having bristles set in a rubber foundation

S

salon stylist: hair stylist employed in a licensed salon

salt and pepper: dark hair having a percentage of white or gray

satisfaction: lives up to expectation

saturation: soaked; completely wet

scatter: to separate randomly

semi-dry: damp; not completely dry

semi-permanent: subject to fading or washing out of the hair gradually without a visible outgrowth

sensitivity: easily offended; very responsive to external conditions

shaping: another term for cutting hair

shaver: instrument used for removing facial hair

shears: instrument having two blades made for haircutting; scissors

shine: brilliance; reflects light

shingle: method of graduating hair lengths from zero to desired lengths, usually at the nap

shorten: to reduce the original length

shrinkage: to become smaller than the original

sideburn: the hair growing on a man's face in front of the ears

skin prep: medicated powder that forms a barrier between the scalp and the base of a hair replacement unit slither stroke of the shears that shortens and thins at the same time

slicing: to make narrow straight parts repeatedly for the purpose of product application

sparse: thin; having less than average

spiral: coiled or coiling in a constantly changing plane

strategically: planned in a precise way to produce exact results

streaks: line or long thin mark differing in color or texture from the surrounding area

stringy: hanging in strings; having no definite form

structural: formation resulting from changes in the original characterization of an object

structured: put together in a concise way

style: part part in the hair that becomes a style detail

styling gel: jelly-like substance used to control the hair during the styling process

styling lotion: liquid having bonding qualities used to control hair during the styling process

subtle: the practice or ability to make a fine distinction

sufficient: as much as needed

surface painting: term given to a technique for applying bleach or tint only to the surface of the hair using a narrow brush

system: arrangement of parts so related as to form a unity creating a whole

T

tailored: sculpted to an exact form

tension: taut; held without slack

texture: the look and feel of hair; the character of a fabric resulting from the arrangement of the particles — fine, coarse, ribbed, ruffled, etc., all can be related to hair

texture shears: shears having notched blades that remove some of the hair at various lengths creating or changing the original texture

texturize: word used to describe the act of adding or changing the texture of hair

thinning: removing bulk from excessively thick hair

towel dry: remove excess moisture from the hair using an absorbent cloth

traveling guide: length of hair that is held as a guide then allowed to drop from the fingers before cutting the hair over the curve of the head

typifies: classic or typical example

U

undercut: the hair is cut very short at the nape; crown hair is left long creating an over-hang

undetectable: cannot be seen

unique: one and only; like no other

unmanageable: cannot be easily controlled

unpretentious: modest; unassuming

untamed: wild; uncontrolled

V

vain: unusual obsession with oneself

variance: degree of change or difference

various: many; undetermined number

vent brush: hair brush having slots in the base through which air can flow

versatile: :that which can be turned or moved around in many ways; ability to move freely

vertex: the highest point; the top

vertically: in a straight up or vertical position

virgin: hair that has not been chemically treated

vogue: fashion

volume: fullness; a quantity, bulk, or amount

W

weaving: a term used to describe a method of attaching a hair extension

weft: something woven; hair to be used in various hair services, i.e., extension, replacement, woven onto a continuous linear base

wefted extension: hair wefts used to extend the length of the natural hair

weight line: point at which the hair falls in one length

working part: part in the hair to be used as a guide while cutting a hair style

Z

zero line: the hair is cut to "zero length" at the nape so no definite line is visible